Francis Smilby

The Canary

Its Varieties, Management and Breeding. Fifth Edition

Francis Smilby

The Canary

Its Varieties, Management and Breeding. Fifth Edition

ISBN/EAN: 9783337139384

Printed in Europe, USA, Canada, Australia, Japan

Cover: Foto ©Andreas Hilbeck / pixelio.de

More available books at **www.hansebooks.com**

THE CANARY

ITS

VARIETIES, MANAGEMENT
AND BREEDING.

WITH

PORTRAITS OF THE AUTHOR'S OWN BIRDS.

BY

THE REV. FRANCIS SMITH,

EDITOR OF "ARMINIUS," ETC.

FIFTH EDITION.

LONDON:
GROOMBRIDGE AND SONS.

M DCCC LXXVIII.

PREFACE.

THE following little Work has been written for the purpose of conveying to the public a somewhat more extensive and accurate knowledge of the many different breeds and beautiful varieties to be found in that most delightful of household pets, the CANARY, than generally appears to exist.

The information given, being "a plain unvarnished tale" of the writer's own personal experience, will, it is hoped, prove alike interesting and instructive to the reader; while the illustrations, drawn by his daughter, being portraits of his own birds, will serve as a guide to those who may wish (like the Author) to form a systematic and choice collection for themselves.

CONTENTS.

CHAPTER IX.

THE CANARY;

ITS

VARIETIES, MANAGEMENT, AND BREEDING.

CHAPTER I.

A PLEA FOR THE CANARY.

"MOST persons," says Mr. Slaney in his interesting outline of the smaller British birds, " are acquainted with three birds—a sparrow, a robin, and a blackbird. Some beside know a skylark; as to the rest, they are often confounded under the general and rather degrading name of small birds. We have sometimes," he continues, " asked our fair friends if they knew as many of the smaller birds as they could count on their fingers! They generally answered confidently in the affirmative, but could seldom get much beyond one hand!"

The ignorance here complained of is not limited to the wild species only, but it is equally true, we fear, of the tame. Take, for example, the subject of the following pages. Everybody supposes that they know a canary when they see it; but bring their knowledge to a practical test by a few plain questions, or set before them a bird whose plumage in any material degree

1

differs from the ordinary yellow bird familiar to us all, and the chances are ten to one that, like the fair friends alluded to by Mr. Slaney, they will soon discover their mistake.   I think I shall not be far wrong when I say that the only idea which most people have of our little favourite is limited to the bare fact that it is a yellow bird having sometimes a patch of black on its head and wings, and singing lustily in its cage.   But never was there a greater mistake.   No bird represents such a variety in its plumage, or exhibits so great a diversity in its shape.   No one, we are bold to affirm, seeing the lizards, the cinnamon, or even a good green bird for the first time, unless a scientific naturalist, would ever dream that they were canaries.

An amusing illustration of the truth of this remark occurred to ourselves only a short time ago.   Having placed a beautiful cinnamon or fawn-coloured bird that we had just purchased and brought home upon the table, a party of ladies soon afterwards called, and became quite enchanted with the singularly delicate hue of its plumage, but never for a moment suspected that it was a canary.   Perceiving their ignorance, some of the children, on their inquiring its name and coun-try, maliciously replied that it was a foreign bird called Sylph, which in one sense was true enough, for I need scarcely tell any of my young readers that canaries came originally from the Fortunate Isles, while the name we had given to the bird in question was, as our youngsters declared, "Sylph."   With this explanation they were perfectly satisfied.   When, after keeping up the joke for some time, you may judge of their surprise on being told that in reality it was only a very common bird called a canary, and that the name we had given it was only its own familiar designation amongst ourselves. Of course they heartily laughed at the deception that had been temporarily practised upon them, and confessed their ignorance upon the subject, though they had all lived in the country, and therefore more or less supposed to be familiar with birds, and what is more, had even been keepers of canaries themselves! The same thing has occurred over and over again with our lizards, and a beautiful wild specimen brought from the island of St. Helena, portraits of which are hereafter given. Indeed, except those engaged in the trade, or in the breeding of prize birds for exhibition, few people are aware of the many very different breeds and beautiful varieties which are to be found amongst these charming birds.

Much has been said and written during the past few years to create a taste for the aquarium and the crawling, cold-blooded inhabitants of the water. With the upper classes there was quite a mania for awhile to make an acquaintance with the stickleback and the newt, and every one was professing an interest in the gyrations of a goggling gulping carp, or the mountebank antics of a lively minnow! Well! chacun à son goût—every one to his taste, as the French say. These, to some minds, may be interesting for a time; but give me an aviary of canaries, whose beautiful colour, elegant form, charming docility, and sweet song, at once charm the eye, delight the ear, and enlist my sympathies! To my mind there is no comparison between the two, and I really wonder the latter has never become the fashion of the day. When canaries were first introduced into England, they were so highly prized that none but the most wealthy could afford to purchase them! In the days of Queen Elizabeth they appear to have been appreciated as they deserved, but in the days of Queen Victoria,—who, however, we believe is a notable exception to the general rule, and who has, we understand, a beautiful collection at Osborne—except by the lower class of people who breed them for sale or show, these beautiful birds seem to be little admired or regarded! How seldom do we see more than one in a house of the middle classes, how rarely do we meet with any number collected together in an aviary or room for the purpose of breeding amongst those who could well afford to do so! Why is this? Has our pretty favourite lost anything of its original beauty of plumage by its domestication amongst us? Is it less elegant in form, less docile in its temper, or less loving and winsome in its manners, than were its progenitors three hundred years ago? By no means; the beauty of its plumage, the elegance of its figure, the docility of its disposition, the charming familiarity which induces it to nestle without fear or reserve beside us, to say nothing of its melodious song which has of late years been well nigh cultivated to perfection, are as striking and prominent as ever. Truly its winsome ways and interesting habits claim and deserve the attention of all classes of society, and if bestowed, we venture to say would unquestionably afford a never-ending round of innocent amusement and delight.

Strange, passing strange, that this beautiful bird is not oftener found in the homes of the middle and upper classes of society than it is. How many a sitting-room opening towards the morning sun, whose walls are now bare of any ornament, either from pictures or bookcase, might be adorned and enlivened by a miniature aviary between the chimney and the window, like the one hereafter to be described. To the sick, or to the invalid obliged to pass the long dreary months of winter within the house, how many an otherwise gloomy hour would their presence lighten, how much interesting occupation and unfatiguing labour would they afford and call into exertion? How attractive and useful, too, wherever there are children, would such an aviary be in a nursery, especially in large towns, where little or no opportunity for studying the habits of birds is presented! To watch them build their nest, patiently brood over their eggs, and hatch and feed their callow young, are operations which are not only intensely interesting to every child, but may be turned with manifest advantage to great practical account. Here they may silently learn those invaluable lessons of kindness, and love, and patience, which shall fit them for the trials of after life, and, it may be, be imprinted on their hearts for ever! Who can tell what consideration for the wants and forbearance with the faults of others these little songsters may be the means of instilling into the youthful mind thus privileged to watch them in their daily course? Who can say what stimulus and encouragement such an aviary might not often afford to the study of every department of natural history, which

but for it might never be undertaken! Seeing and
knowing little, many a child, we feel assured, would
naturally be led to desire to know more. Books thereon,
as a natural consequence, would be sought after with
avidity, and read with profit and delight, which but for
the canaries might probably lie idle and unlooked into
on the shelf. As the cost is so trifling, the pleasure so
great, the interest never ceasing, and the effect so good,
we feel persuaded that the idea only requires to be suggested for many to carry it out in practice in their nur-
series and homes. At any rate, should any be led to
make the experiment, we can promise them a golden
mine of amusement and delight, which those who have
never tried it would little credit or suspect. As Robert
Nicholl sang of its kindred finch—the linnet—so may
we, with equal or greater truth, say of the canary:

> "Some humble heart is sore and sick with grief,
> And straight thou camest with thy gentle song,
> To wile the sufferer from its hate or wrong,
> By bringing nature's love to his relief.
> Thou churmest by the sick child's window long
> Till aching pain itself be wooed to sleep;
> And when away have vanished flower and leaf,
> Thy lonely wailing voice for them doth weep—
>   Linnet, wild linnet!

> "God saw how much of woe, and grief, and care,
> Man's faults and follies on the earth would make;
> And thee, sweet singer, for His creature's sake,
> He sent to warble wildly everywhere,
> And by our souls to love to wake.
> Oh! blessed wandering spirit! unto thee
> Pure hearts are knit, as unto things too fair
> And good and beautiful of earth to be—
>   Linnet! wild linnet!"

CHAPTER II.

ORIGIN OF OUR OWN CANARIA.

IKE many a greater undertaking, our canaria had its origin in a very small beginning. Its first traces, I believe, are to be found in a well-meant gift of a kind granny to my daughter Judy, who, I may as well say, once for all, was evidently " born to love pigs and poultry," and which consisted of a common yellow canary purchased in the market of my native town. Had I been able to foresee the result of this very questionable action, it is more than likely that I should have exclaimed, with Mr. Jorrocks, of famous fox-hunting celebrity and renown :—" Confound all pre-sents wot eats ;" while she, I think, would hardly have consented to be the innocent cause of such a large expenditure in cages, birds, and seed, as that which has since taken place. Happily, however, for Judy, I was no seer, and granny was not gifted, like the famous heroine of Lucknow, with second sight. The purchase was made on the eve of our return home from an annual visit we pay into " the shires ;" and back dicky was brought to the smoky city of Manchester, where for many years it was our lot to be located. Of this bird I remember little, save that he was a good yellow, pos-sessed a very amiable disposition, and was a most uproarious songster. Indeed, so noisy was he during lessons, that my wife was obliged to cover his cage with a cloth before ever she began to teach, which the chil-dren, of course, voted a great shame. He lived a bachelor's life, all alone, for about three years, when he died in moulting, whilst we were all away from home in the autumn, probably from neglect, being left in charge of a servant, who knew little and cared less about the requirements of birds under these trying circumstances. Great was the grief amongst our youngsters at this untoward event, for such a thing as his dying had never entered their heads, and they probably expected that he would live for ever. To soothe their grief and repair the loss, on a fine Saturday morning towards the end of October, I and the three elder children, having set out on our usual marketing expedition, paid a sauntering visit to the bird fanciers' stalls. Here we loitered about for some time, more out of curiosity than with any idea of buying, when we suddenly found ourselves standing before an old man's cage, who soon endeavoured to turn the occasion to account by soliciting our attention to the quality of his wares, and setting them off to the best advantage he could. Though the day was somewhat cold and bleak, and the birds were starved, we saw enough to make us listen to his tale, and finally to make a purchase of what seemed to us then a pretty little curiously-marked grey hen canary, but about which I shall have more to speak in another chapter, leaving behind another singularly coloured companion, which, after all, perhaps, was the prettier, and certainly the more rare bird of the two. The one we purchased was, to a fancier's eye, by no means a good specimen of her kind, her feathers being all tipped with white, which they should not be, and her general colour being, instead of pure grey, tinged here and there with a yellowish green. Still, for all that, she was a very pretty bird, and we were all highly delighted with her purchase. We took her home, as usual, in a little paper bag, which, I may observe, is by far the best way of carrying a bird you purchase without a cage, and always to be had at the nearest grocer's shop, when she evinced a most amiable disposition, and soon became as tame as our original dickey himself. Having thus got a hen canary, the idea not very unnaturally occurred, how nice it would be to have some young ones! The thought was so captivating to the youngsters, that it soon took firm hold of their minds, and culminated into an intense desire to make the attempt. But how was this to be done? Our house was so small, and our family so large, there was no room for such a thing, seeing that canaries, when breeding, require not only a goodly space, but plenty of light, and perfect quiet. The only room in the house fit for the purpose was clearly the children's nursery, and the place where the birds ought to be was already taken up with bookshelves, on which were piled, besides books, innumerable boxes and toys, including a four-roomed doll's house, which they had made and fitted up out of so many old tea-chests they had begged for the purpose, and which almost reached up to the ceiling. Well, what was to become of these? There was no other visible place for them in the nursery. Oh, this should be no obstacle in the way, they replied, if I would only let them have an aviary, and remove the books to the other side of the room, they would do all the rest. Their much-loved doll's house should be stowed away in their bedroom, and all the other boxes should be put into drawers at once, if I would only consent. Well, I thought, the thing is feasible, and will please me almost as much as the children. So we set to work with a hearty good will; the things were soon stowed away and the bookshelves put up elsewhere, leaving two of the latter to form the floor and top of our proposed aviary. I then ordered a piece of nicely-tinned wirework, four feet ten inches long by two and a half feet deep, to be made, having three sliding doors, so placed as that one should be in the centre near the bottom, and one near the top at either end, so that the birds might be readily cleaned and fed, and their nest-boxes be changed when required. And now we were all impatience to begin. The wire was faithfully promised by the end of the week; but, alas! Saturday arrived, and yet no appearance of any wire. Off we set the first thing on Monday morning, to know the reason why, when again it was faithfully promised the next day. That day came, and another, and another, but still no wire. A second Saturday night, and we felt sure it would come. Every footstep that passed by the street-door was listened to with bated breath, and every rap sent the hearts of the children, who were now wound up to the highest pitch of excitement, straight into their mouth; but still all ended in disappointment, and they were again obliged to go to bed without that long-expected wire. A second Monday sees us at the rascally wire-maker's door, who we now discover to have been all along paying his devotions to his favourite god Bacchus, and too fuddled with drink to work. This

was past all endurance, so we left word that if it was
not completed and brought home by the next day, we
should give the order to some one else, which at once
produced the desired result. The wire arrived late one
night, and I was fain to buckle to, and put it up at
once, for until this was done the children, I soon saw,
would let me have no peace.

Although abhorring all manual labour from my
youth, and seldom taking a tool in my hands, lest, as
they say of the monkeys and their talking, I should be
made to work, I accordingly commenced my task.
Though a seemingly simple operation, it took me longer
than I expected, so that the children had to be sent off
to bed in the middle of the work ; and it was nearly
twelve o'clock before I had brought my labours to an
end. Two shelves of wood, little more than a foot wide,
and four feet six inches long, placed against the wall
between the chimney corner and a large bay window
opening to the morning sun, formed the floor and roof
of our miniature aviary ; four narrow iron stanchions
placed at equal distances apart, form so many supports
for the latter, and at the same time tend to strengthen
the wirework to which they are bound ; and thus the
whole thing is complete for the trifling sum of twelve
shillings.

On coming down stairs the next morning, the children
were enchanted at the sight. The long-wished-for desire
of their hearts was no longer an airy vision of the imagination, like the castles and palaces of some fairy tale,
but a great reality. Aladdin himself could not have
been more delighted with the view of his enchanted

palace than were they with the vision of this palatial residence for their dickies. The long-drawn lines of the brightly-tinned wire shining in the morning sun, contrasting in strong relief with the dark iron stanchions to which the wire was bound, gave a charm and airy lightness to the whole, which exceeded the utmost bounds of their conception. They at once expressed intense satisfaction and delight at this happy realisation of their wishes, which thus formed a handsome, spacious, and useful aviary, at a very trifling cost, fit for the habitation of the very choicest specimens of canary land.

To transfer the birds to their new habitation, and see how they would look, was but the work of a few minutes; and the only regret was we had not another above it. This, we all thought, would not only be extremely useful for the birds, but greatly improve the appearance of the whole. As it would only require another shelf, and a piece of wirework similar to the other, we decided at once to double the size of our aviary, which accordingly was soon done.

As all would clearly have to be taken down and re-arranged, we think it would decidedly add to the beauty of the whole, if in place of the dark claret-coloured paper with which the wall at the back was then covered, a light blue marble-coloured paper was substituted instead. This we thought would certainly contrast better with, and set off to greater advantage, the yellow plumage of the birds, as well as make it more cheerful and light. Accordingly, having procured the necessary paper, to my other accomplishments I add that of paperhanger for the nonce, with Judy for my help. Though I had not served a regular apprenticeship to the trade, I never doubted for a moment but that we should soon accomplish the task, and was somewhat surprised to find out that, like many other things in the world, it was not so easy as it seemed.

The woodwork being put up first, it seemed the quickest and most natural way to cut the paper the whole length required at once, rather than into a number of short strips from the roof to the floor. This I accordingly did; and having often seen how the regular practitioners paste a whole piece before putting it on the wall, I thought I would do the same. So, spreading my paper on the window-seat, I soon put on the necessary paste to my complete satisfaction. Thus far all was well, and I had only to put it up against the wall close by and dab it down with a cloth. But, alas! how true is the saying, "There's many a slip between the cup and the lip." Taking hold of the upper corner of one end, Judy doing the same at the other, I just succeeded in raising it to the desired place, when, horror of horrors! the whole, from its weight, gave way in our hands, tearing in all directions. As fast as we attempted to save one part, another began to go; our fingers thus got all over paste, and we made an awful mess of the little we managed to preserve, till at length, seeing the hopelessness of our task, we gave it up as a bad job, when a general collapse ensuing, the whole mass fell to the ground in one irreparable heap of rubbish and ruin! Here was a practical proof, indeed, of the proof of the proverb which says, "the more haste,

the worst speed," at the same time that it showed us
what is very often hard to believe, viz., that we were not
quite so clever as we thought. Though certainly dis-
comfited, we were not dismayed, but gaining wisdom by
experience, we manfully set about our work again,
singing the while—

> " The web 'mong the leaves
> The spider weaves
> Is like the gay charm Hope hangs o'er men;
> Though often she sees
> 'Tis broke by the breeze,
> She spins the bright tissue again."

Instead, however, of trying to do it all at once, we
cut our paper according to the depth required. These
short lengths were soon put up by mamma, who now
came to our aid. Slips of plate-glass, about two inches
deep, were fitted inside the bottom of the wirework, so
as to take out at pleasure, through which the birds
looked very pretty, and could always be seen, whilst they
kept the sand and seed from falling out and being
scattered about the room. A cut-glass vase, in each
compartment, to hold their water to drink, and to bathe
in, gave additional lustre to the whole, which, thus
finished, became quite as ornamental to the room as it
was useful for the purpose we intended.

Having thus completed our aviary, we naturally
began to wonder how many young ones we should
have, how pretty they would look just popping their
heads over the sides of their nest, and how charming it
would be to see them first hop abroad in the world.
Already visions of profit began to rise before our eyes
as we began to calculate the numbers we should have

to dispose of, and the prices they would unquestionably fetch. Supposing, we argued, we had four pairs of birds in each aviary, and each pair bred twice a year only, and reared four young birds each time, a very moderate calculation, we considered, seeing that many writers put them down as breeding generally three and sometimes four times a season, and having five and six at a brood, and supposing that each pair only fetched five shillings, then it was pretty clear that we should not only pay our expenses, but realise a considerable profit besides. Thus, like the enthusiastic milkmaid in the fable, did we hoist our basket of eggs upon our heads, and count our chickens before they were hatched. The birds, however, were not yet bought that were to produce these golden dreams; and the question was, how and by whom the necessary capital was to be raised. Judy, as the owner of dicky, wanted to go shares with me in all that were bought, so that she might have an interest in each pair, and share in the profits they were to bring. Agnes was of the same mind, and wished to do the same, while Gerty was in-different, Letty too prudent, and poor Polly, as usual, unable. This, however, I thought would dip too deeply into their exchequer; so I compromised the matter by allowing the two former to advance ten shillings each from their own funds, and to beg another ten for the purpose from their granny, and I would find the remain-der, the whole to be divided into so many shares, accord-ing to the capital ultimately required, and each receiving a proportionate amount of the profits that should be made. Thus Judy, Agnes, and myself, entered into a sort of joint-stock partnership with limited liability for the purpose of breeding canaries—an arrangement which suited all parties, and gave great satisfaction to each. The firm being thus completed, we entered upon the business with great zest, having full confidence in the soundness of our project, and deriving from it much immediate pleasure, which was certain to increase as the spring came on, if it did not actually realise our most sanguine expectations of profit.

> " Where is the troubled heart consigned to share
>   Tumultuous toils, or solitary care,
>   Unblest by visionary thoughts that stray
>   To count the joys of fortune's better day ?
>   Oh ! vainly wise, the moral muse hath sung,
>   That suasive hope hath but a syren tongue !
>   True, she may sport with life's untutor'd day,
>   Nor heed the solace of its last decay ;
>   The guileless heart her happy mansion spun,
>   And part, like Ajut, never to return !

> " And yet methinks, when wisdom shall assuage
>   The grief and passions of our greener age,
>   Though dull the close of life, and far away
>   Each flower that hailed the dawning of the day ;
>   Yet o'er her lovely hopes, that once were dear,
>   The time-taught spirit, pensive, not severe,
>   With milder griefs her aged eye shall fill,
>   And weep their falsehood, though she loves them still."

CHAPTER III.

THE WILD CANARY—THE EMPEROR.

THE picture on the opposite page is an accurate drawing, both as to form and colour, of a beautiful wild canary now in our aviary, and which, from his being brought from the island of St. Helena, we call the Emperor. He has now just got over his second autumnal moulting, and, to a casual observer bears little resemblance to the ordinary yellow domesticated bird, with which we are all familiar. His beak and legs are shining black, and much more powerful than those in the tame species, as he will soon let you know if you take him in your hand. His body also is much stouter, approaching more the fulness of the linnet than the tapering slenderness of the golden-yellow birds bred in England and Belgium. No one, looking at him for the first time, would suppose that the bright grass green of his back, with darker wing coverts and tail, had any alliance with any of the varieties commonly found at home. Yet such is the case. All writers agree that their natural colour is a greyish brown, merging into yellowish green in the under parts of the body. "In their native state," says a writer in the ' Popular Cyclopædia,' "they are of a dull and uniform green, and exhibit none of that richness and variety which are so much admired in the tame ones." Our bird is anything but dull in his colours ; on the contrary, both the green on his back and the yellow of his belly are of

2

the most vivid kind, the former not having the least mixture of brown usually found in the green birds bred at home. His song, too, is entirely different from the tame variety, nothing like so loud or piercing, but more approaching the subdued warbling of the gold-finch or linnet. Indeed it is acknowledged on all hands, that the song of our domesticated birds is alto-gether artificial, being little else than a compound of notes learned from other birds.

It was about the beginning of the sixteenth century that the canary became first known in Europe, when a ship having a large number on board, and destined for Leghorn, was wrecked on the coast of Italy. The birds having regained their liberty, flew to the nearest land, which happened to be the island of Elba, where they found so mild a climate that they built their nests there, and became very numerous. But the desire to possess such beautiful songsters led to their being hunted after, until the whole wild race was quite destroyed. In Italy, therefore, we find the first tame canaries, and here they are still reared in great numbers. Their original locality, however, was the Canary Isles, from whence, I suppose, they derive their name On the banks of small streams, in the pleasant valleys of these lovely islands, they build their nest in the branches of the orange-trees, of which they are exceeding fond; as an instance of this, even in this country birds have been known to find their way into the greenhouse, and select the fork of one of the branches of the orange-tree on which to build their nest, seeming to be pleased with the sweet perfume of its blossoms.

As they are naturally inhabitants of warm climates, and made still more delicate by constant residence in rooms, it is of the highest importance to keep these birds in a warm equable temperature during winter, and free from all cold draughts of air in summer, two hours' exposure to the latter either in summer or winter being sufficient not only to cause sickness, but certain death. To keep canaries in a healthy and happy state, it is desirable that the cage should be frequently hung in brilliant day-light, or, if in a room, that it should open towards the morning sun, which especially they delight in, and which when bathing is as necessary as it is agreeable to them.

So attractive has been found the canary on account of its pretty form and charming qualities of its mind, that it is now kept and reared throughout the whole of Europe, and even in Russia and Siberia. Indeed, as Beckstein has justly remarked, " the qualities of its mind are as varied, or even more so than its plumage, for amongst them it has been discovered, as amongst quadrupeds and even men, some individuals are gay, and others melancholy ; some quarrelsome, others mild ; some intelligent, others stupid ; some with quick memories, others lazy ; some greedy, others frugal ; some petulant, others gentle ; some ardent, others cold." Our own aviary amply bears out this statement, and proves what an infinite fund of pleasing recreation and instructive amusement a very small collection of these very beautiful birds will afford. Thus Buttercup is the gayest of the gay, whilst Daisy will sit and mope upon her perch for hours together, immoveable as " patience upon a monument smiling at grief." Lady Grey is amiability itself, whilst Spangle, her lord and master, is irascible and fierce as the baron of Shurland Castle when he called for his wondrous boots. Dandy is energetic, as Sultan is portly and sedate. Marquis is mild and gentle, whilst Prince Charming is the essence of good breeding and propriety. Little Brilliant is lazy and greedy, as Blanche is quick and the Princess *distingué* in her breeding. Seraph has a wonderfully retentive memory, having learnt many of the notes of the German canaries in whose company he was but a few days. In short, each bird has its own characteristic individuality, and is a study in itself, ever varying in its mood with the changing circumstances of the hour. In sunshine gay, in winter dull, in spring-time full of life and vigour, in autumn moulting, and sick, and weak; when courting the most ardent of lovers, when married the most dutiful and affectionate of husbands, helping their wives with the most assiduous attention when making their nest, and superintending the bringing up and education of their family with exemplary regularity and care, now receiving some delicate morsel from their owner's hand, and then showing their gratitude by repaying him with a song. Such are some of the many attractive qualities of the canary, such are the traits of character which our own present to our daily notice. The reader, therefore, may judge for himself whether we have overrated the merits of these charming birds, or can possibly be wrong in thus recommending them to the more favorable notice of the public.

"Birds! birds! ye are beautiful things,
  With your earth-treading feet, and your cloud-cleaving wings;
  Where shall man wander, and where shall he dwell,
  Beautiful birds, that ye come not as well?
  Ye have nests on the mountain, all rugged and stark,
  Ye have nests in the forest, all tangled and dark;
  Ye build and ye brood 'neath the cottager's eaves,
  And ye sleep on the sod 'mid the bonnie green leaves;
  Ye hide in the heather, ye lurk in the brake,
  Ye dive in the sweet flags that shadow the lake;
  Ye skim where the stream parts the orchard-decked land,
  Ye dance where the foam sweeps the desolate strand.
  Beautiful birds! ye come thickly around,
  When the bud's on the branch and the snow's on the ground;
  Ye come when the richest of roses flush out,
  And ye come when the yellow leaf eddies about.
  Beautiful birds! how the schoolboy remembers
  The warblers that chorused his holiday time;
  The robin that chirped in the frosty Decembers;
  The blackbird that whistled through flower-crown'd June.
  That schoolboy remembers his holiday ramble,
  When he pulled every blossom of palm he could see,
  When his finger was raised as he stopped in the bramble,
  With 'Hark! there's the cuckoo; how close he must be!'"

CHAPTER IV.

OUR LIZARDS.

S O great has been the effect of domestication, and the pains that have been taken in their breeding, that canaries may now be found of almost every hue and colour. "Buffon enumerates twenty varieties," says a writer in the 'Popular Encyclopædia,' "and many more," he continues, "might probably be added to the list, were all the changes incident to a state of domestication carefully noted." We know not how these gentle-men would classify them, or what difference is sufficient, in their estimation, to constitute a distinct variety. Many, we imagine, would be but slight modifications of the same general colour, and could scarcely be anything more than slight and fanciful variations at the most. For our own part, we think the following will include most of those which have any claim to be considered a distinct variety, and even these will be found in breeding to produce birds quite different in colour to themselves, so that the variety spoken of is rather to be understood as an accidental circumstance belonging only to the individual bird, than as referring to any difference in the breed to which it may thus chance to belong. Setting aside the wild canary, we have the well-defined lizards, the Yorkshire spangles, the Norwich golden yellows, the London orange, with black wings and tail, the green, the cinnamon or fawn, the buff or pale yellow, the pure white, the orange Belgian, and the German, and under one or other of these heads all the rest may be ranged. As we have specimens of all these varieties in our own aviary, we shall say a few words upon each, and Judy will give accurate portraits of the birds, which together we hope may prove both instructive and interesting to all who may honour our pages with a perusal.

Curiously enough, the first bird that we purchased was, perhaps, the most rare, as certainly it is the most distinct variety, viz., the Lizard, so called from some fancied resemblance in its markings to the reptile of that name. The coloured representations on the opposite page are very fair likenesses, and convey a very good idea of a pair of our own birds, whose history I will now relate. Were they not told beforehand, few people, I think, would take them for canaries, which thus bears out the assertion I made at the beginning of the book as to the general ignorance which prevails amongst people unconnected with the trade, and shows at a glance what a variety there is amongst them.

It was on a fine November morning, now some years ago, that Judy and I started off to a well-known bird-dealer's, to make our first purchase for the new aviary. We set out with the intention of buying a pair of the London variety, which, however, we found not to be much in request amongst the bird-fanciers of Lancashire, and therefore seldom to be met with in Manchester. The nearest approach to anything of the kind we saw was a bird of a golden-yellow colour, with black spots or stripes on the crown of his head. As he was a lively, elegant-shaped bird, though somewhat weakly and very young, we soon had him separated from his companions, and hung in a black show-cage for our inspection. With good keep and careful attention we thought he would soon outgrow these deficiencies, and as we otherwise thought him a desirable bird, there we left him, whilst we looked round the stock in the adjoining room, and finally determined on the propriety of his purchase.

Here, amongst others, we saw a whole cage-full of that charming variety called the Lizard, but whose markings remind me much more of the gold and silver-pencilled Hamburg fowl, or Sebright's bantam, so well

known amongst poultry, as will be seen from our illustration. Their distinguishing characteristic consists in
having the crown of the head, either pure white or
yellow, like the tonsure of a Cistercian monk, whilst
the rest of the upper part of their bodies are covered
all over with regular black spots on a clear grey or
bright orange, after the manner of the fowls above
alluded to. The tail, wings, and feet should be of a
uniform dark hue, without any admixture of white,
while the throat and breast should be of a lighter shade
and approach more nearly the colour of the head.

It so happened that in the cage before us were some
particularly good specimens of the kind, and I need
hardly say we were delighted with our visit. As yet,
however, we had no idea of making a purchase, believing
them to be altogether out of our reach, and so we told
the dealer at once, and were about to pass on. This,
however, he would not hear of, no doubt thinking that,
like the clockmaker and his clocks, if he could only
gain a hearing, he might safely trust to human nature
to finish the bargain. So taking a slight wand in his
hand, he soon separated from out of some twenty or
thirty others one of the finest birds he had in the
room. Placing him in a jet black cage upon the table,
with the rays of the morning sun shining brightly on
his plumage, he required no Yankee soft sawder to
commend him in our eyes. Judy was enchanted, I was
delighted. What could we do? One of the most
splendid coloured and regularly-marked birds our eyes
had ever beheld, now sat proudly on his perch, and
demanded at our hands the homage he evidently felt

due to his rank and birth. Could we help inquiring about his price? Had the most phlegmatic spectator or the most inveterate bird-hater been placed in our position, we think he could not have done less. "Well, what will you take for him?" we timidly ask, more by way of gratifying our curiosity than with any real intention of buying. "Ten shillings," is the reply. Ah! this is beyond our mark, for as yet we have not made up our minds to go beyond half that sum. The bird, we acknowledge, is dog-cheap at the money, and we both sigh that we cannot afford to give so much for a canary. With longing eyes and lingering steps we turn our backs upon this most beautiful of birds, and return to complete the purchase of the one we had left in the adjoining room. Judy remained transfixed with enchantment to the spot whilst our purchase was effected, which caused another visit to the room, and ended in a sort of wavering in our hitherto stoical determination to resist all temptation to buy. But alas! for our pocket, we are charmed with the voice of the charmer. The tempter approaches us in the shape of a whisper from Judy that he is so beautiful, she will give half the sum required out of her own pocket, if I will only consent to the purchase; already we begin to give way, when reason steps in with the conclusive argument, that if we really intend to breed canaries, we may as well breed good ones as bad ones, seeing that the difference is only in the first cost. This clenched the matter at once, we listened to the pleasing delusion and fell willing victims, I fear, to the temptation we at first so manfully resisted. Judy carried him home

delighted beyond measure with our success, but judge
of our astonishment and dismay when, on first exhibiting our splendid prize, he only met with qualified
admiration and praise. From want of eyes to see, and
knowledge and taste to appreciate our illustrious
stranger's beauty, some said he was only "very well,"
while Agnes, whose taste is generally very good, openly
declared, "there was nothing to make such a fuss
about" in him! How it was they failed to see him in
the same light that we did, when we first saw him in
the dealer's shop, I cannot tell, but we consoled ourselves with the reflection, that it was "useless to throw
pearls before swine," whilst they now confess with
Judy and myself that truly he is a beauteous bird.

The first hen we bought of this breed, and which,
like the one in our picture, was a light grey, came to
an unfortunate and untimely end, which, inasmuch as
it may serve as a caution to others, I may as well
relate. Being of a very tame and amiable disposition,
she naturally became quite a pet with the children, and
soon learned to leave her cage and fly about the nursery,
and perch upon their hand without the smallest fear.
Every day, as soon as they came home from school, the
cage-doors were immediately opened, and out flew the
birds, which thus had their liberty for several hours
a day, much to our youngsters' admiration and delight.
Unfortunately birds were not the only pets in the house,
for Judy had another in the shape of a very fine large
grey tabby tom cat, whom for his noble appearance and
many good qualities she has named after the greatest
of Roman generals, "Drusus." Whether he merits so

honorable a title, however, may fairly be doubted, for
he is undoubtedly a great thief, and not very scrupu-
lous in the means he employs to obtain his own ends.
Indeed, he is not to be trusted, though very aristocratic
in his outward appearance, and wearing an enormous
moustache, a bit farther than he can· be seen, and
scarcely that. .In an evil hour the children, having let
out their birds as usual, thought, as the little redpoles
were rather troublesome to get in again, they would
leave them at large whilst they had their dinner in the
parlour. This they accordingly did, when all of a
sudden in comes the cook, and announces, without the
least concern, in her dry Lancashire way, " T'cat's got
a bird," and again as quietly retiring; she and the
nurse immediately sat down to their dinner without
making the least attempt at a rescue. Not so we. Out
we all moved; but, alas! too late, as you may suppose,
to be of any avail. As soon as he had seized his prey,
Drusus retreated to his lair in the cellar, where we
could hear him growling and swearing at the bottom of
the steps. After him went Judy and Gerty, who soon
found him with the bird in his mouth; the latter, un-
deterred by the danger, dashed upon him at once, and
rescued the poor victim from his ferocious grasp. But
the deed was done — our much-prized little lizard
canary was no more; and all we could do was to lament
over our loss, and scold the servants for their careless-
ness in leaving the door open, and their unfeeling con-
duct in selfishly sitting down to their own dinner,
instead of trying to save the life of the bird ere it was
too late. The accident, however, has been a warning

to us since ; and we never let any of our birds out unless
some of us are present to keep watch and guard against
the enemy.   Cats and birds are naturally mortal foes,
and should never be in the same room, or even house,
together.

But having now got a splendid cock bird, if we were
to breed pure lizards, we must necessarily purchase
another hen.   This, of course, necessitated another visit
to the dealer in question, to see if we could get a mate
worthy of our former purchase, and at the same time be
within the limits of our purse.   In this we fortunately
succeeded, purchasing a beautiful grey hen without a
foul feather about her, and which had already been
paired with the bird we had previously bought.   To a
person unacquainted with the subject of breeding the
canary it may seem strange that I should select a grey
hen to pair with a yellow cock.   To obtain brilliant-
coloured birds it might have been thought that a hen
similar to the cock would have been most likely to
ensure the desired effect.   I confess that I was of this
opinion myself at first, but was assured by practical
breeders and fanciers that the latter method is the most
approved fashion, and that birds of opposite colours invariably produce young with the finest feathers and
markings.

Having got the birds, the next thing was to find
them appropriate names.   As now we were going to have
a numerous family, it became absolutely essential to
give each its peculiar name, in order to distinguish the
one from the other.   After tea, therefore, a grand pala-
ver was held on the hearth-rug, Indian fashion, before

the fire, to determine this important point. It was unanimously agreed that the name to be adopted should be easy of pronunciation, expressive of their peculiar character, or a tribute to their beauty. Many were the names suggested, and many were the objections raised to their adoption. High-sounding titles of Spanish chivalry, or of Arthur's princely court, or German fairyland, failed in the triple requisition we had conceived necessary for such an illustrious pair. Names renowned in Roman history or Grecian song shared no better fate, till at last some one hit upon the simple but expressive titles of " Spangle and Lady Grey," which all acknowledged to be so peculiarly appropriate and characteristic, that they were at once unanimously adopted. We hope, therefore, our readers will recognise the propriety of their names, and think with us that a baronet's title well became the beauty and rank of a pair destined to take so high a position in canarian life.

> " What's in a name ? That which we call a rose
> By any other name would smell as sweet;
> So Romeo would, were he not Romeo call'd,
> Retain that dear perfection which he owes,
> Without that title."

CHAPTER V.

OUR YORKSHIRE SPANGLES AND NORWICH YELLOW.

HESE two varieties represent the ordinary description of canary to be found more or less in almost every town in England. They are respectively so called from the places where each is chiefly bred, and usually found in the greatest abundance.   Our representation gives a very fair idea of the general character of each, and will show the difference of the two at a glance.   The spangled bird, usually of a pale mealy colour, with greenish-brown head and wings, is the more general favorite with the working men in the manufacturing district of Yorkshire and the north, whilst the golden yellow is preferred by the men in the neighbourhood of Norwich, where it is chiefly bred, and from whence it is annually sent up in large numbers for the London market.   The former is much the more robust and stronger bird of the two, but of course lacks that beautiful golden plumage which gives such an elegant and airy lightness so striking in the appearance of the latter.   The Yorkshire bird, too, say the Lancashire fanciers, is superior in its song ; but this, for my own part, I very much doubt.   I do not profess to be a judge in this matter ; but, so far as my experience and observation go, I should certainly have awarded the palm in this respect to the bird from Norwich.   They are certainly more sprightly and energetic, and more vigorous and constant in their song, than their brethren of the north, who are necessarily, from their shape and constitution, generally speaking, of a more phlegmatic temperament.   The Norwich bird, no doubt, is more nervous, and consequently more delicate in his constitution ; but he makes up for this, in my opinion, not only by the superior beauty of his colour, but by the greater vivacity of all his movements, and the hearty, merry joyousness of his song.   To see

him dance along his perch, merry as a grig, and beating
time to his own tune, as with distended throat and up-
raised crest he pours out a torrent of sweet song, capti-
vates you at once, and makes you a sharer of his joy.
To me the Yorkshire birds always seem deficient in these
points, and give you an idea of a steady, dull plodding
man, very excellent in his way, but never electrifying
you with the brilliancy of his thoughts, or thrilling you
with the fiery energy of his action. This, however, may
be mere fancy on my part, but so it is. I admit being
partial to colour and vivacity of action, whether it be
found in fish, flesh, or fowl. Being more accustomed to
the golden yellow of the south-eastern counties, I may be
no impartial witness in the matter; but, however this
may be, still I say "the yellow-haired laddie" for
me !

The breeding of canaries by the working classes
in the manufacturing districts we have named is
not only a very favorite pursuit, but a very profitable trade. The numbers which they annually breed,
and the prices which they will give for a good
canary, will appear fabulous, and altogether unjusti-
fiable, to those unacquainted with the subject. Our
artisans in Manchester think nothing of giving one,
two, and three pounds for a single bird. On a
Saturday afternoon and night the market and shops,
as well as the public-houses used for the purpose,
are crowded with men and lads, having either birds
to sell, or looking on and watching what is going
on around them. The veriest tyro in the business
thinks as little of giving five or ten shillings for a

bird as he does of giving eightpence for a pound of steak to frizzle with his tea. The late disastrous crisis through the want of cotton has dealt a hard blow to the bird-fanciers in this locality, many of whom were of course entirely out of work. Very pitiable was it to see a man or lad obliged to part with the pets of his household through sheer want, and then, when the birds were gone, selling the empty cage as well. I myself lately, more out of charity than because I really wanted it, gave a poor lad from Stockport five shillings for his cage, after he had sold his birds in the market, to support his family, who were literally starving for the want of food. Still it is astonishing to see the numbers yet kept. In almost every other house, I had nearly said in every back street in Manchester, when the cottage-doors were open, you might see breeding cages hanging on the walls, and hear their occupants enlivening the gloomy desolation around. During the darkest phase of the distress a poor woman, whom I was visiting in order to relieve, and who nevertheless was in great distress herself, on my pointing to a canary which hung in what had once been a very handsome cage, and inquiring how she could afford to keep a bird, when she could not keep herself, replied, with tears in her eyes, "Ah! sir, that bird was my poor husband's. Poor fellow, he gave fifteen shillings for it, and five for the bird, which I thought sadly much of at the time; but it was his only hobby, and I keep it for his sake. The poor thing is getting old now, and does not sing so well as it did; but I would sooner part with anything I have in the house than it or the cage." I admired her for

the self-denial and feeling love which she thus mani-
fested in her widowhood and distress for the aged songster, who thus recalled the recollection of better times
and brighter hopes, and gladly gave her a portion of
that bounty which had been entrusted to my charge.
So far as I could see, it appeared to be

" The one green spot in her memory's waste,"

and long may it be ere this remaining link in her life's
existence be severed from her grasp. How sweetly does
Mrs. Hemans sing those alone can understand who,
like Byron, have felt solitary " amidst the crowd and
hum and shock of men :

"Give me but
Something whereunto I may bind my heart,
Something to love, to rest upon—to clasp
Affection's tendrils round!"

This is no solitary instance. The poor bird will often,
we feel convinced, be the last thing parted with by
those long-enduring and heroically patient men. Any-
how, the breeding of them is, as we have said, an
enthusiastic and often profitable pursuit. Exhibitions
are held and prizes are given by societies formed for the
purpose, which, as the 'Times' lately remarked, is a
vast step in the way of civilisation, and infinitely in
advance of the cock-fighting and bull-baiting of former
days. For lack of support by the upper classes of
society, and for want of suitable room anywhere else,
I am sorry to say these are chiefly held at some public-
house or tavern, whose landlord finds it to his interest
to give a considerable sum, that the meetings may be
held at his house. Thus I have now before me a bill

3

announcing a grand annual show of Belgian canaries, which was to take place last Whit-Saturday, at a certain public-house in this town, whose landlord gives £4 10s., on condition that the show is held at his house, that he have the appointment of the judges, that the birds shown remain for exhibition until the night following the day of showing—which, of course, is Sunday—and that every member spend 6d. each monthly meeting night, which, I am sorry to add, is also on a Sunday, previous to the show, whether he be present or not.

Now, objectionable as much of this is, it is worse than useless to rail at the amusements of the people, unless we provide them with others equally attractive. By a little countenance from the classes above them, and by a little judicious management and attention, surely a recreation so harmless in itself might be divested of the attendant evils at present surrounding it, and made subservient to the education and refinement of the people. The free use of one or more rooms connected with our public institutions, and the giving of a few pounds towards the prizes, like the worldly-wise publican above, would surely induce these poor men to hold their meetings during the week day, and leave the Sabbath for bodily rest and spiritual sustenance of their soul. By so doing, I, for my part, cannot but believe that much would be done towards counteracting the attractions of the public-house and its attendant evils, much towards enabling the working classes to overcome the pernicious habit of frequenting them, much towards fostering in their breasts a love for healthier and purer

scenes, much towards making them feel that there was
a time for all things, and that the Sabbath most
assuredly belonged to the Lord their God.   The exhibition and breeding of these beautiful birds is certainly
a pursuit to be encouraged; and I believe that if the
religious portion of the community would only encourage
these and such like innocent and rational modes of
amusement among the working classes, the latter would
not be long insensible to the kindness and sympathy
shown in their behalf.   By degrees they would be re-
claimed from the haunts of vice and crime; by degrees
they would imitate the example of those above them;
by degrees they would be found filling our churches
and keeping the Sabbath, as it should be kept by every
man professing to be a Christian, "holy unto the Lord."
As William Cowper truly sings:

> " Religion does not censure or exclude
> Unnumbered pleasures harmlessly pursued;
> To study, culture, and with artful toil
> To meliorate and turn the stubborn soil;
> To give dissimilar yet fruitful lands
> The grain or herb, or plant that each demands;
> To cherish virtue in an humble state,
> And share the joys your bounty may create:
> * * * * * *
> These, these are arts pursued without a crime,
> That leave no stain upon the wing of time."

CHAPTER VI.

OUR LONDON FANCY BIRDS.

F all the varieties of the canary, perhaps this is the most beautiful of any. It is known in the trade as the London fancy, because it is there that it is chiefly bred. They are of a rich golden yellow or deep orange, with black wings and tail, like the bird represented on the opposite page. About their breeding there is much mystery and some peculiarity which fanciers like to keep to themselves. To get into these secrets is almost, if not quite, as difficult a matter as to penetrate into the mysteries of training a race-horse for the Derby or St. Leger. One thing is certain, that to produce them in a state fit for exhibition at the annual show at Sydenham, as much training and attention, united with skill, is required as is necessary to bring a high-bred racer to the post. Not only must the bird be fed on the most nutritious and dainty food, but the sides of his cage must be encased with glass to shade him from every draught of wind; and he must be kept at a high temperature, like the race-horse, to produce that condition and glossiness in his plumage which shall enable his owner to obtain the prize. That it is strictly a cross-bred bird I have no doubt, inasmuch as there is this peculiarity about it, that when quite young it is mottled all over on the back something after the fashion of a Lizard, and that it only acquires its clear golden yellow after its moulting, and then retains only the pure black of its wings and tail the first year. The

second autumnal moulting introduces white or grey into
these latter, which at once disqualifies it for the purposes of exhibition, and increases year by year till it
becomes merely an ordinary plain bird we see every
day. To be a prize bird there must not be a foul
feather—that is, either white amongst the black, or
black or grey amongst the yellow, found in its body.
The latter also must be a rich golden yellow or deep
orange, without any approach to a paler or mealy tinge,
which at once would be fatal to its chance of success
when exhibited in competition with others. Such being
the case, we need scarcely say that a bird possessing
such qualifications is comparatively rare, and fetches a
high price. A guinea and upwards is the ordinary
price asked by dealers for these beautiful specimens of
canary land, though good birds, with here and there a
foul marking disqualifying them for exhibition, may
often be purchased for half that sum. For my own
part, I believe this beautiful variety has been produced
by crossing a Lizard cock with a French hen, whose
colour is a beautiful bright yellow, with an intermixture
of jet-black spots, and but little or no white in them—
a variety which was first introduced into this country
some few years ago, or *vice versâ*, as the case may be. By
judicious crossing and recrossing in this way, I have no
doubt the London fancy bird of which we are speaking
has been obtained and preserved; and any one fond of
making experiments of this nature so doing would, I
feel persuaded, be rewarded with success for his pains.
This, however, it must be understood is merely a private
opinion of my own, countenanced, nevertheless, by men

well versed in the breeding of birds here; for, as I said before, those engaged in the matter are very mysterious about their operations, and little inclined to impart their secret to the world.

Well, our great desire now was to obtain a pair of this beautiful variety for our aviary. This was brought about by reading in the newspapers of the day an account of the beautiful birds exhibited at the Sydenham show, and seeing a picture of this lovely variety in the work of a popular author of the day, which also informed us that it was almost peculiar to London and its vicinity. I now recollected that I once myself bred a single brood having jet black wings, tail, and head, from a pair of apparently common-looking birds, which my brother brought home when he came from Harrow School, and which were the most beautiful of any I had ever then seen. Unfortunately, however, they all met with a sad fate, and I never succeeded in rearing any more of the kind. Being so exceedingly beautiful I brought them from the room in which they were bred, and placed them in a large cage which stood in our entrance-hall, on a pedestal for the purpose. As might naturally be expected they were the admiration, if not envy, of all who saw them, but alas! this did not last long, for one night either a mouse or rat got into the cage, and killed every bird in it, so that when the servant opened the shutters in the morning, there was nothing but a few feathers and mangled remains of the poor little things left. It was a sad misfortune, and grieved us all very much at the time, but it was one which we could not have foreseen, and scarcely have provided against. When there is any suspicion that there is any such vermin about, care should be taken not to place the cage against anything by which they may climb up, or a fate similar to that which befel our birds will assuredly be the consequence. The best plan, where practicable, is to hang the cage on a hook for the purpose in the ceiling, which precludes the possibility of accidents of this nature, and places them at once beyond the reach of danger.

Many years had passed since then, and I had never seen any canaries either like my own or those depicted and described as being now exhibited at the Crystal Palace, and peculiar to London. In vain I inquired for them in Manchester, in vain I asked where they were to be obtained, the only response being that they were seldom seen anywhere but at the great shows held in the metropolis, where they were highly prized. Judge then of my delight when, one day calling at our bird-dealer's shop for some seed, he told me he had two or three birds of the London breed down at his other place, in another part of the town. Thither I accordingly repaired, and soon descried three splendid-coloured birds in a cage in the shop-window; two of them were somewhat irregularly marked, but one answered my purpose in every respect, being of a beautiful golden yellow or orange, with black wings and tail, and having only a very faint tinge of grey on one side of his neck. I at once determined to secure him, but unfortunately the man left in charge of the shop was gone out, and there was only a little girl, who knew nothing about the price, in. Dinner-time was fast approaching, and I could not wait till his return, and so I reluctantly left the bird behind, not daring to say anything about his purchase until I knew his price.

I carried the news home, however, which immediately created the intensest excitement amongst the children. It would never do to let such an opportunity pass by, without attempting to buy him. Judy urged that immediate steps should be taken in the matter, lest some one else should step in, and deprive us of our much-coveted prize. This we thought not at all unlikely, and so decided to return immediately after dinner, for the purpose of seeing, at all events, whether he was within the reach of our pockets, if we did not actually buy. Dinner, as might have been expected, now became of little consequence in their eyes, the meal was soon despatched, and Judy and I started upon the exciting errand. Though it was a dark sombre afternoon, and more than two miles and a half off, we started very willingly in a thick drizzling rain to purchase this much-desired and lovely specimen of canaria. Before we arrived at our journey's end the wind blew quite a hurricane, and the rain poured down, whilst many were the misgivings we had by the way, lest, after all, our labour should be lost, and the bird be gone. With as much joy as feels the tempest-tossed mariner who sees the friendly port, and descries the haven where he would be, we at last reached our destination, and found the birds were still there. Judy was enchanted, the price moderate, the opportunity favorable, so we were not long in securing the great object of our search. We chose the more regularly marked bird of the three

for a cock, and a mealy hen, according to general recommendation, with a dark-crested head, for his companion, which we put into two paper-bags, and started
back on our return. But the wind again blew a hurricane, and the rain poured down incessantly, so that
Judy and I could hardly make head against it. To
secure the birds, therefore, from the violence of the
tempest, I transferred them to my hat, which I pressed
firmly on my head. In this way we wended our weary
uphill way back, bravely bearing up against the pitiless
storm, and darkening night, caring little for either
wind or weather. Though the distance was full five
miles, Judy declared she would have walked twice as
much, rather than have lost the chance of securing such
a prize. At length we reached home, where a cheerful
fire and comfortable tea were awaiting our arrival,
and made us soon forget all the discomforts of our
journey.

Before bit or drop, however, was tasted, a host of
inquiries had to be answered, and the eyes of the ex-
pectant group, who now gathered clamorously around
us to know the result of our expedition, must be
gratified! No sooner did they see the well-known
little bags produced than, as might have been anticipated, their anxiety knew no bounds, to catch a
glimpse of the expected prize! Every foot-fall for
some time had been listened to with anxious expecta-
tion, and now they could wait no longer. So whilst
we pull off our wet clothes, they willingly prepare a
cage, and into it we soon turn our much-prized treasures. The rich plumage of the one, and the sprightly

liveliness of the other, at once captivated all hearts, so
that Agnes at once bestowed upon them the very
appropriate names of Brilliant and Beauty, which they
have ever since retained, and still deserve. But, alas,
the former is evidently all the worse for his journey; he
sets up his feathers, and rolls about the bottom of the
cage like a drunken man; with great difficulty he can
sit upon his perch, and it is plain, from some cause or
other, that he is very ill altogether. Though his case
looked bad, and there was obviously considerable danger
of our labour being lost by his death, mamma could
not help joking us about the loss of our money, and
the enthusiasm we had displayed. We were in no
mind, however, to lose him so easily, or to give him up
without making an attempt to cure him of his malady.
Judging that he had been made giddy by the length of
his journey, and the close confinement and want of
air he must necessarily have experienced in my hat, I
immediately took down my homœopathic medicine-
chest, and prescribed what I thought would be likely
to suit his case. Mixing four or five drops of tincture
of belladonna in his water, I placed it in his cage, when
he immediately freely and frequently drank of its
contents, which seemed to revive and bring him about
at once. By degrees he became able to retain his seat
on the perch, so that by the time we went to bed we
had little or no anxiety about his recovering. The
next morning he was evidently much better, though
still far from well. We continued, therefore, his medicine, changing it in a day or two to china in order to
recruit his strength, when, after a little time, I am

glad to say, "Richard was himself again." It was a narrow escape certainly, and I would advise every one to be cautious in putting a bird into their hats for any long distance. The practice, I know, is very common, and answers very well for a short journey, and where there is plenty of ventilation, but it becomes dangerous when either the distance is long, or the ventilation stopped or imperfect. We had now, however, got our heart's great desire, and the portraits we have given of the birds themselves will show that their beauty is not over-rated, and that we did well to encounter so long and rough a journey for their acquisition. We knew full well the value of opportunity, and profited by our knowledge. The lesson this little incident may teach we hope will not be lost upon our youthful readers, for most assuredly, as Shakespeare sings—

> "There is a tide in the affairs of men
> Which, taken at the flood, leads on to fortune;
> Omitted, all the voyage of their life
> Is bound in shallows and in miseries.
> On such a full sea are we now afloat;
> And we must take the current when it serves,
> Or lose our ventures."

CHAPTER VII.

OUR BELGIANS.

HAVING thus secured a pair of Lizards, a pair of Yorkshire spangles, and a pair of London fancy birds, we were no longer satisfied with the little short, ill-shaped, common canary usually met with, but raised our thoughts at still higher game. Christmas had now arrived, and brought with it the usual foreign importations from Belgium and Germany. Accordingly, one bright December morning, Agnes and I set off to our bird-dealer's to see what there was to be seen. There we found a numerous and splendid collection of beautiful and high-priced birds from Belgium awaiting our inspection, and with whose lovely colour and noble bearing we were at once delighted. There was as much difference between these birds and an ordinary English canary as there is between an old-fashioned Northamptonshire cart-horse and a pure bred Arabian of the desert. Nor is the comparison inappropriate; on the contrary, it serves to point out the essential differences existing between them. Thus, as in the horse, so in the bird, whereas the head of the more common breed is thick, and round, and narrow, that of the Belgian is square, and wide, and flat, the skull and back forming an exact triangle, instead of the narrow oval usually found in the foreheads of the common breed; whereas the neck and throat of our English birds are short, and thick, and clumsy-looking, that of the Belgians is long, tapering, and elegant; whereas the whole body of the former is short and stumpy, that of the latter is long, tapering, and slender; whereas the colour of the former is, comparatively speaking, poor and mealy (we are speaking now only of the common varieties), that of the latter is rich, and bright, and pure, many of them presenting as much difference in the matter of colour as exists between a ripe orange and an ordinary lemon. The great feature, however, that distinguishes this elegant breed from all others is their high square shoulders, and erect position when standing on their perch as represented in our illustration. This gives them a remarkable and peculiar appearance, which is produced by the pinions of their wings being placed higher up on their backs than those of any other variety, and which thus consequently distinguishes them from all others.

Though so much esteemed by Fanciers, and fetching far higher prices than any other breed, it is surprising how seldom and briefly they are mentioned by those who have written specially upon the subject. Bechstein says literally nothing about them at all, whilst all the authors of the present day it has been our fortune to meet with, either follow his example, or their remarks are so short and so general, if not absolutely untrue, that it is clear they can have little practical acquaintance with this department of their subject. Thus, a popular London writer who was, at one time, regarded as a great authority on the subject, writes thus, " Of late years the Belgian canaries have come into repute with some fanciers. They are long-bodied, and anything but elegant in form and carriage. They are, however, strong, healthy birds, and by pairing a cock of that breed with a Norfolk or Yorkshire hen, which is of a more compact shape for sitting on the eggs, a fine race is the issue. Their song does not excel that of the breeds just mentioned, but they assist in forming a variety." Having thus oracularly delivered himself he then dismisses the whole subject as unworthy any further notice whatever. Now, if we state that the reverse of all this is the case, we shall be simply stating the truth, as our readers will gather from the description and illustration already before them. The Belgian, instead of being, as this author describes them, "anything but elegant in form and carriage," is, on the contrary, extremely and necessarily elegant, not only in the outline of his figure, but when animated or excited also in the bearing of his carriage. Drawing a line from the point of his beak, over the crown of his head, taking in the curve of his neck, and the rise of his shoulders, and proceeding down his back to the tip end of his tail, he presents a series of curves as nearly as possible approaching to that waving line of beauty which Hogarth, in his ideal of elegance, sketched upon his palette. View him as you will, from above or below, from his shoulders or his chest, the lines become "fine by degrees and beautifully less," utterly forbidding any loop-hole of escape in the oft-repeated but false dictum that, after all, "such things are a mere matter of taste." Beauty of form indeed is a matter of taste, but not of fanciful taste or mere whim and caprice, and is as much regulated by well-defined and well-understood laws as any which regulate any other matter of art or science. Had the writer in question, however, stopped here, no great harm would have been done, as people in this matter could judge for themselves; but when he goes on to say that "they are, however, strong healthy birds," he says that which is the reverse of true, and which, in the nature of things, is calculated to lead people astray. So far from their being anything of the kind, I believe every bird-dealer in the kingdom who

has had any experience in the matter, will bear me out
when I say, that of all the various breeds as yet introduced into our country, the Belgian is by far the
most tender of any. Indeed it requires no great knowledge of physical anatomy to understand that such, from
the conformation of the bird, must necessarily be the
case. The extreme narrowness of their chest absolutely precludes them from being otherwise than very
delicate, for to be healthy and strong, we all know, a
wide expansion of chest is absolutely requisite in bird,
beast, and man. In this there can be neither exception
nor qualification ; to talk therefore of their being either
" strong " or " healthy " is simply ridiculous, and
betrays not only great ignorance, but almost makes us
doubt whether a man so talking could ever have seen
one in his life. My own experience has already confirmed what reason and information had already told
me was the case, and I repeat again that of all the
various breeds of the canary hitherto known in this
country, that of the Belgian is the most tender and
delicate to manage of any.

Well, a splendid show of these remarkable birds had
just been imported direct by our bird merchant, who
goes himself periodically to make their selection. Where
all is beautiful it is difficult to make a choice, and this
time Agnes and I felt very much like the ass between
two bundles of hay recorded in the fable ; our choice,
however, was not so extensive as it seemed, for, besides
the beauty of the birds their price also had to be considered, and this had a considerable influence in guiding
us to a choice. Indeed, this was the greatest obstacle

in our way, for, in reply to our inquiry into this rather delicate affair, we were very politely told that our friend had nothing under thirty shillings apiece in this cage, and that, while for particular individuals he should want two, three, and as much as five and eight pounds each! At this we opened our eyes, and stared rather widely, as you may suppose, not being as yet prepared to give more than as many shillings for a canary. To our untutored eyes there was little apparent difference among them, but that there was such we had convincing demonstration by seeing several ordinary working mechanics come in, and, picking them out, give their two and three pounds for a bird, without the least demur or hesitation. In fact, Mr. M— assured me that he had just sold three birds at the respective prices of five, eight, and nine pounds each, whilst he had known as much as twenty-four pounds sterling to be given for one in its native country. Such prices, I need scarcely say, did not suit our pocket, and were given only for birds specially designed for exhibition. He had, however, others, which he had taken in exchange for those newly imported, and which he could sell much cheaper; so with these we were fain to be content. Half a dozen birds of this description, and which for the purposes of breeding were, perhaps, little inferior to their higher-priced brethren, were soon separated by the aid of his magician wand from the rest, and drafted out from a host of others into as many little black cages for our inspection. Proudly did they stretch out their long thin necks and snake-like heads, as they stood erect upon their perches, demanding our homage! Truly, it was a beauteous sight. Agnes was at once all eyes, whilst I was in raptures of delight! This bird excelled in form, that in the richness of his colour, a third had a finer carriage, a fourth a greater development of the shoulder, a fifth is more animated in his movements, whilst a sixth is more lengthy and taper in his body. How shall we decide? Among such a profusion of charms, how make a selection? Agnes goes for elegance of figure. I am captivated with the colour. She pleads for a tapering figure. I insist upon squareness of head and development of shoulder. Minutely do we scan their respective beauties, and canvass their various charms. At length we compromise the matter by choosing a very lengthy hen and a deep golden-coloured cock with a beautiful snake-formed head, high shoulders, and deep body, for which we give the comparatively small sum of fifteen shillings the two. Home we carry them, highly pleased at the success of our mission and the cheapness of our bargain. Of all the Christmas shows we had yet seen this eclipsed all; nothing in the way of feathers, we thought, could ever come up to it. To transfer them to their new abode was but the work of a few minutes on arriving at home: the next thing was to cast about for names befitting their high dignity and station. Towering far above all others, and excelling them in the gorgeous richness of their yellow plumage as much as do the beams of the morning sun the calmer rays of the queen of night, we at once placed them in the regal rank. There being no others to dispute their possession to the royal throne, they were at once admitted to their new palace, amidst a general chorus of

4

song and twitterings of delight, where they reigned as the undisputed "Sultan" and "Sultana" of their race.

"And let the good be named 'The Good;'
　The true, 'The True;' the brave, 'The Brave;'—
Titles not bought and sold for blood,
　Like those our war-girt monarchs gave—
And let the just be still 'The Just,'
So men shall know wherein they trust.

"Look on our noble once again,—
　None nobler graced the ranks of old;
No death-strewn fields his honours stain;
　He battles not for fame nor gold;
But with an earnest, loving heart,
He cometh still, and plays his part.

"No painted badge, no tinsel star,
　Lie idly glittering on his breast;
But—nobler, grander, worthier far—
　Truth's light stands in his eyes confest;
And round the broad brow proudly plays,
That glows and brightens in its blaze!

"This brave, high homage, spirit-paid,
　Shall shrine the worth of woman too,
Fitly entitling wife and maid,
　'The Meek,' 'The Tender,' or 'The True,'
And she whose brow small beauty wears,
May yet well grace the name she bears.

"Is this a dream?　No!—by the past,
　With its dense darkness—pierced at length—
And by the present—brightening fast—
　And by the future's noon-day strength,
Earth's truly Great and Good shall be
Her last, best aristocracy!"

CHAPTER VIII.

OUR GREEN BIRDS.

AVING thus got so many distinct varieties of breed, we now desire to add to our little collection specimens of every description of colour. In our Yorkshire and Norwich birds we had the spangled white and plain yellow, in the lizards the dark grey and green gold, in the London fancy the rich yellow contrasting with the jet black, and in our Belgians the pure golden orange. There were two others we particularly desired to meet with, viz., a pure grass green and the exquisite fawn. With regard to the first of these we did not suppose we should have much trouble, though in this we were destined to be deceived; whilst with regard to the latter we stood in considerable doubts whether we should be able to obtain one at all, as we knew it to be the rarest of any. Though green birds are as plentiful as blackberries, they were all, we soon found, more of a dingy brown than a real green, and for the most part very ugly, ill-shaped birds, into the bargain. Scores and scores did we see with heads and necks thick as those of the common house-sparrow, and whose plumage was more like that of the linnet than a canary. With such short, stumpy, ill-favoured, and dingy-feathered birds we would have nothing to do. When we said we wanted a green canary, we meant one whose colour was as green as the grass or the leaf of an ash-tree, coupled with a form long, tapering, and slender as that of the Belgian. On this we had set our

minds, and this or none we would have.   Long had we
to wait, many a journey into the bird-market on a
Saturday morning, and many a look into the bird-
dealers' shop-windows did we take before we could
meet with one anything approaching to the idea we had
in our mind's eye.   At length Mr. M— had a batch of
the description we were in search of, and we had the
first pick of the lot; unfortunately there were no hens,
but all cocks.   We soon, however, made our choice, for
our eye immediately fell on a bird which united in himself all the qualifications we required.   Brilliant in
colour, snake-like in head, and lengthy and tapering in
body, as well as animated and lively in his movements,
we soon saw he would be all that we could desire.   He
was as unlike the ordinary birds of his kind we had
hitherto seen offered for sale as it is possible for two birds
of the same species to be.   There was not the slightest
resemblance to the linnet-like tribe we have described;
but his elegant form and vivid colour at once proclaimed
his near alliance to the Belgian blood.   Strutting about
in his bright green coat, interlaced with long dark
stripes down the back, and in his vest of saffron-yellow,
no sooner was he introduced to the palace of the sultan
than his high breeding was recognised at once, and he
became quite the exquisite of the court.   On this
account we gave him the name of "Dandy," from the
somewhat foppish character of his gait, though he is by
no means effeminate; on the contrary, he is robust and
energetic in all his actions, foremost in every fray, sings
a capital song, is very sociable in his disposition, and
quite a jovial character every way.   Every one thought

him quite an acquisition to our select circle of canaria, where his striking appearance makes him ever the observed of all observers.

It was again a long time before we could find a spouse fit for so beautiful a bird. Many were the visits we paid to the market, many were the peeps we took at the bird-shops, ere we could meet with a hen to our liking. At length, however, we met with one quite accidentally, as we were passing by the arches under the railway station on the London Road, where my ear was suddenly attracted by the well-known "sound as of many waters," from a hundred little German throats, and which told me that a fresh arrival of canaries had taken place. Soon I espied a window full of those little wooden cages in which these charming songsters are annually imported into this country, and below them one or two apparently English-bred birds, which induced me to enter. The place was stifling hot, being purposely so kept by means of a stove, in order to make the German birds maintain a continual gush of song during the short time their wandering proprietor might stay, but which, I need scarcely say, is a practice no less contrary to nature than it is injurious to the bird, and the cause of much complaint and disappointment to the purchaser. The effect already produced on some of the English birds was plainly perceptible, and many of them looked languid and drooping, from the great heat to which they were exposed. Among them, however, were two birds which, from their colour, I particularly desired to possess, one of which was a green hen, exactly answering the description of bird we wanted as a mate for our bachelor "Dandy." She was a beautiful dark grass-green, with well-defined clear black markings down the back, and without a white feather about her at the time. I say at the time emphatically, for I afterwards discovered one had been plucked from her tail by the crafty German, in order to enhance her value in the eyes of an unwary purchaser. This trick is a very common one, I believe, with low, unprincipled dealers, who besides often paint their birds into the bargain, so that it requires a very practised eye to detect the imposition. In London, I am told, this very reprehensible practice is carried to a great extent, even by dealers of long standing and position, and who would be very much surprised and highly indignant if they were told they were neither honest nor respectable! Yet such is the fact, and I mention it, not only to put the unwary on their guard, but to call the attention of such dealers and the public to the subject, that the one may be ashamed of its publicity, and the other exercise its power to put it down.

But to return. The bird before us, besides being suitable for our purpose as regarded her colour, was equally so in point of breeding and shape. Like that of her destined lord, the elegance of her figure, the fineness of her head, and the length of her body, bespoke at once her alliance to the Belgian strain. She, however, looked languid and drooping, which, though I knew was the effect of the high temperature of the room, still made me hesitate about her purchase. It was in vain that they assured me in the shop she was quite well and in perfect health, for my eyes told me at a glance that she was nothing of the sort. There she sat languid and listless on her perch, evidently quite overpowered by the heat, if not absolutely ill from other causes. Still the German stuck to his text, or rather her text, for it was a woman I had to do with, and to every objection that I advanced she made a counter-assertion in the opposition direction. So, like the man who goes into a horse-dealer's yard, and ventures to think that the animal he is shown turns *in* his toes a trifle too much, and is shut up at once by the fierce off-hand dictum of the dealer that so far from anything of the sort, that worthy thinks if there is any fault at all in this respect he rather turns them *out*, I began to think that perhaps after all there was not much in it, and so concluded the purchase. On my way home, however, I called and showed her to Mr. M——, mentioning my suspicions, which he immediately confirmed on taking her into his hand, from her feeling soft and spongy, instead of firm and hard to the touch, as a bird in good health and condition invariably is. My worst fears were soon verified on our arrival at home, when she had to be consigned to the hospital at once, instead of being introduced to her intended lord, for whom she would otherwise have been a most excellent match. I kept her some time during the winter, and tried every remedy I could think of to cure her, but she proved in the end asthmatical and finally died after I had parted with her in the spring.

Thus we wasted our time, and lost our money, and were no forwarder than when we first began our search for a mate worthy the exquisite Dandy. Winter passed and spring came, without our seeing another at all suitable as his match, and we began to despair of ever meeting with a bird of the description we wanted, when one morning Judy and I casually called at Mr. M—'s to see if anything fresh had come in, and met with the thing we desired. He had just received two well-bred green birds from the country without a foul feather about them. We chose the neatest and most sprightly of the two, and immediately introduced her to her future lord, who took to her at once, and seemed highly pleased with our choice. Though a beautiful little bird, and a great favourite with us all, she has never arrived at the dignity of a name, which she certainly ought to have had, but continues to this day to be known only by the title of " the little green hen." For this, however, she is none the worse, she makes Dandy an excellent little wife, and is as exemplary as she is beautiful. By way of concluding the present subject, let us listen therefore to the excellent advice so charmingly given by Edwin Henry Burrington in a volume entitled ' Revelations of the Beautiful '—

" Walk with the Beautiful and with the Grand,
 Let nothing on the earth thy feet deter;
Sorrow may lead thee weeping by the hand,
 But give not all the bosom-thoughts to her;
  Walk with the Beautiful.

" I hear thee say, ' The Beautiful '! what is it?
 O, thou art darkly ignorant! Be sure
'Tis no long weary road its form to visit,
 For thou canst make it smile beside thy door;
  Then love the Beautiful!

"Ay, love it; 'tis a sister that will bless,
    And teach thee patience when the heart is lonely;
  The angels love it, for they wear its dress,
    And thou art made a little lower only:
               Then love the Beautiful!

"Sigh for it;—clasp it when 'tis in thy way!
    Be its idolator, as of a maiden!
  Thy parents bent to it, and more than they;
    Be thou its worshipper. Another Eden
              Comes with the Beautiful!

"Some boast its presence in a Grecian face;
    Some, on a favourite warbler of the skies!
  But be not fool'd! Where'er thine eyes might trace,
    Seeking the Beautiful, it will arise!
              Then seek it everywhere.

"Thy bosom is its merit, the workmen are
    Thy thoughts, and they must coin for thee: believing
  The beautiful exists in every star,
    Thou mak'st it so; and art thyself deceiving,
              If otherwise thy faith.

"Thou seest Beauty in the violet's cup;—
    I'll teach thee miracles! Walk on this heath,
  And say to the *neglected flower*, ' Look up,
    And be thou Beautiful!' If thou hast faith,
              It will obey thy word.

"One thing I warn thee: bow no knee to gold;
    Less innocent it makes the guileless tongue,
  It turns the feelings prematurely old;
    And they who keep their best affections young,
              Best love the Beautiful!"

CHAPTER IX.

OUR CINNAMONS.

THE first cinnamon, or fawn-coloured canary we ever saw, was one in the old bird-fancier's cage who stood in the market at the time of our visit recorded in our second chapter. At that time we had not yet formed any definite idea in our minds as to breeding, or indeed of having an aviary at all. But now this had taken place, and become as the French say *un fait accompli*, we sorely regretted the opportunity we had missed in not making a purchase. As our plan of operations developed itself, and breeds of different localities and countries, as well as varieties of colour, were decided upon, we sighed to think that we might never have such a chance again. Weeks and months passed on without our seeing anything of the kind, when, calling one day at Mr. M—'s shop, what should we see in a cage just brought in by a countryman for sale, but the very bird we had let slip in the market some months before ! Here was a piece of good luck, I thought, which could never have been expected ! Unfortunately, however, Mr. M— was out of town, and the stranger had only contingently offered the birds for sale in a lot, and had now departed. As he was an entire stranger, and they knew neither his name nor address, I left word with the man in charge of the shop to be sure and tell Mr. M— to buy the cinnamon bird specially for me. The next day we all

went down to look at this charming bird again, and highly delighted we all were at the thought she would soon be our own, as we did not doubt about easily coming to terms as to her price. The day following Mr. M— had returned, but the owner of the birds had not been. Saturday, and he was sure to come, when our fondest wishes would be realised! Judge then of our disappointment when, on calling the first thing on Monday morning, we heard that Mr. M— had not been able to comply with our wishes, as the man insisted that all his birds were cocks, whereas Mr. M— considered them to be all hens, which made a considerable difference in their value! The worst of it was the man was quite a stranger to Mr. M— also, who knew not who he was, or where he came from, and now the birds were gone, and our much coveted cinnamon was, to all appearance, a second time, if not for ever, again beyond our reach! Great was the lamentation over this mishap; Mr. M— tried to console our chagrin by telling us the bird would have done us no good, as it had been kept in too warm a place, and was already beginning to moult, and consequently would not breed this season. No doubt what he said was in some measure true, but we felt it was but sorry comfort after all. We had set our hearts upon having so rare and beautiful a specimen of canaria, and just as we thought we had secured the prize there came the unexpected "slip betwixt the cup and the lip!"

Time passed on, but instead of bringing balm to our wounded feelings, it rather increased our grief. The more we thought about the matter, the more beautiful did our imagination paint the lost one in our eyes, and the more convinced we became that we should never look upon her like again. We tried to think that as there was " more fish still in the sea than ever came out of it," so it might be with the feathered tribe, and we might therefore yet retrieve our loss. Weeks glided away when, passing down a street in a distant part of the town bent on other business, Judy and I espied another bird-dealer's shop, when the thought occurred to us to inquire if they had any cinnamon canaries on sale. At first the reply was in the negative, but on our lingering and repeating the question, the man began to scratch his head, and think over the matter, and then turning short round, and reaching down a cage full of birds immediately behind him, he added in a way that gave us to understand he should not give himself much trouble about the matter, he thought there was a hen of this kind among them, which assuredly there was. The birds were wretchedly dirty and looked very miserable and forlorn through long neglect, but a glance showed us the bird we were in search of. There could be no mistake about the matter. Though she was now quite changed and hardly recognisable from filth, we felt sure that it was the very bird we had seen at Mr. M—'s shop, and in the market some weeks before, as she had a peculiar narrow white stripe at the back of her head, something like that of a young cuckoo. Judy recognised her at once, but prudently kept her own counsel, only giving me a significant look and nudge. Besides, on closely inspecting the others we further recognised two of her companions as well, so

without betraying our inexpressible delight, we carelessly asked the price, which was now only two shillings.
We made a slight demur on account of the wretchedness
of her condition, and bid eighteenpence, but seeing the
man would not take less, and that he had actually put
the birds back again on the shelf, we at length gave an
apparently reluctant assent to his terms, though nothing
was further from our thoughts than a third time losing
the opportunity of securing such a prize. We threw
down the money on the counter, and the bird was soon
put into a bag, when Judy and I hastened out of the
shop with mutual congratulations on our good luck.
Not only had we got the bird we had so much desired,
but we had obtained her at a less price than we could
have bought her at Mr. M—'s, or in the market where
we had first seen her.

> "She was a phantom of delight
>   When first she gleamed upon my sight;
>   A lovely apparition, sent
>   To be a moment's ornament;
>   Her eyes as stars of twilight fair;
>   Like twilight too, her dusky hair;
>   But all things else about her drawn,
>   From May-time and the cheerful dawn;
>   A dancing shape, an image gay,
>   To haunt, to startle, and waylay."

It was some time before I could meet with a mate
suitable for this beautiful and peculiar-coloured bird.
We saw four or five at various times, but they were all
very common-bred, ill-shaped birds, and nothing
approaching to the delicate shade of our own bird. At
length I met with a strong, healthy bird, handsomely

marked, and of the colour required, at the German
store alluded to in the preceding chapter. He was not
altogether what I should have liked, being pied instead
of self-coloured like the hen we possessed. Still he
was a very handsome bird, very evenly marked on his
head, back, and wings, with a reddish fawn, with a
white body, set off with patches of golden yellow on his
cheeks, throat and rump. He was said to have been
bred in Yorkshire, which is very probable, as I have
since learned that Barnsley is known among dealers as
the place of all others where this particular variety is
bred. Although he had been only a few days among
the Germans, so apt was he at learning, and so retentive his memory, that he acquired a considerable portion
of their peculiar song, which he sings most lustily with
his own at this present time. From the beauty and
excellence of his song, and the delicate hue of his
plumage, we named him Seraph and his wife Sylph,
and a charming and very singular variety of the canary
they are! Take them away from their well-known
brethren, and place them in a cage by themselves in
any drawing-room in England, and very few of our
lady visitors, we will venture to say, would ever dream
of their being of the same kith and kin as the yellow
specimen so familiar to us all. Whence, then, it may
naturally be asked, comes this great difference, and how
has it been brought about? We candidly admit we do
not know. All that we can say is that the original
stock was of a uniform green, as we have already stated
in another chapter, and that the rest are in some way
the result of its domestication. A short glance, how-

ever, of the several theories advanced by various writers
may be neither uninteresting nor unprofitable to my
young readers, whilst at the same time it may set them
thinking upon a subject which has perplexed much wiser
heads than our own, and if it serve no other purpose,
this will be an advantage in itself.

About the origin of these several varieties and great
difference of colour found in the canary much diversity
of opinion, as might naturally be expected from a subject
so obscure, exists. Some ascribe it to locality, others
to food, and others again to cross-breeding with birds
of a kindred tribe. Thus Adamson, in support of the
former of these ideas, says, " I have observed that the
canary, which becomes white in France, is at Teneriffe
of a grey, almost as dark as that of a linnet." Again,
Beckstein says that " the grey of its primitive colour
darker on the back and greener on the belly, has
undergone so many changes from its being domesticated,
from the climate, and from the union with birds ana-
logous to it (in Italy with the citril-finch, the serin ;
in our country [that is, Germany] with the linnet, the
green-finch, the siskin, and the goldfinch), that now we
have canaries of all colours. If we had not sufficient
proof that canaries came originally from the Fortunate
Islands, we should think that the citril-finch, the serin,
and the siskin, were the wild stock of this domesticated
race. I have seen a bird, whose parent birds were a
siskin and serin, which perfectly resembled a variety of
the canary, which is called the green. I have also seen
mules from a female grey canary in which was no trace
of their true parentage. The grey, the yellow, the

white, the blackish, and the chesnut, are the principal
varieties, and it is from their combination and from
their tints that we derive the numerous varieties that we
now possess." Others again would ascribe the difference to a difference of food, saying that some birds
fed entirely upon hemp-seed have been known to lose
their natural colour, and to become black, and that
such was proved to be the fact most conclusively by an
experiment made upon a nest of young bullfinches, who
grew up to be entirely black instead of their usual
varied plumage. These gentlemen forget, however,
because it is not convenient to remember, that in the
case thus so conclusively cited the birds on the very
first moulting, after they had had different food, at once
regained their natural colour, and thus really demon-
strated the fallacy of the theory which they were at first
supposed to substantiate.

That these and all similar notions have not the least
foundation in fact, it will be sufficient to observe that
the wild birds themselves vary almost as much as the
domestic, and yet have necessarily the same food, and
that in reality there is no bird in a domesticated state
whose food is less various than that of the canary in
every country where it is known. But even were
such not the case, we challenge the authors and sup-
porters of such a fanciful notion to produce a single
instance in either bird or beast where any particular
food has been known either to change white into yellow,
yellow into green, or green into grey, or grey into
chesnut, or produced stripes in one case and spots in
another. The idea is really too absurd, we think, to be

entertained for a moment by any one laying claim to the title of a rational creature.

Equally erroneous is the idea of climate or locality having anything to do with the matter. As in the case of the food, so it may be answered, all the varieties are found in every climate and country, and not separately in each. The yellow, the grey, and the chesnut, as well as the green and the white, are found as often in Russia as they are in Italy, or France, or England. Climate, therefore, cannot have any influence in this respect upon the bird, any more than it has upon man himself. " Place an Anglo-Saxon," says a well-known writer on the various races of men,* " with his flaxen hair and blue eyes under the most burning sun, and no length of time will change him or his offspring into a negro. The Saxon of to-day is identical with the Saxon of the most ancient times. They follow the law of hereditary descent ; climate exercises no influence over them. Two hundred years of Java, three hundred years of Southern Africa affect them not ; alter their health it may, it does, withering up the frame, rendering the body thin and juiceless, wasting the adipose cellular tissue, relaxing the muscles and injuring the complexion by altering the condition of the blood and secretions ; all this may be admitted, but they produce no permanent results. The Saxon is fair, not because he lives in a temperate or cold climate, but because he is a Saxon. The Esquimaux are nearly black, yet they live amidst eternal snows ; the Tasmanian is, if possible, darker than the Negro, under a climate as mild as

* Dr. Knox.

England. Climate has no influence in permanently altering the varieties or races of men; destroy them it may and does, but it cannot convert them into any other race." Now if this be true, as we think it unquestionably is, in the case of man, it must be equally true of the feathered tribes in general, and of the canary in particular. Climate, therefore, we repeat cannot have anything to do with the alteration of their plumage, any more than the food which they eat, and to which, it must again be observed, they are all equally exposed alike.

Still more preposterous is the idea that all this variety in their colour has been produced by cross-breeding with other varieties of the Finch tribe. We do not doubt for a moment the possibility of breeding a mule between a canary and a linnet, a canary and a goldfinch, or a canary and a siskin, for we ourselves have both seen and done it. Nor do we doubt that occasionally cases may be found where these hybrids have bred again, for the Rev. Mr. Wood, in his delightful book entitled 'My Feathered Friends,' gives the result of two interesting experiments he made upon the subject, and in which he succeeded in obtaining a young bird from a hybrid canary-goldfinch paired with a pure hen canary, and also another from a pair who were themselves both hybrids. But still, what we say is this, that these are only to be regarded as exceptions to the general rule and law of nature, and that their very rarity only makes the rule the stronger. There is no abrogation, and never can be, of that wise law which Providence has ordained alike for every animal under the sun, and which restricts species to species and stamps sterility on every hybrid. If there be one thing more certain than another, it is undoubtedly the fact that there is no such thing to be found in nature as a hybrid or mixed race springing up, and becoming a permanent variety. Even in the case of man, with all the arts and appliances of civilisation, and therefore with the most favorable circumstances to aid him, it has ever been found impossible. After a few generations they either die out altogether, or the dominant race regains its natural purity. How much less, then, can we suppose such a thing to have taken place in the case of the canary, delicate and tender as it is by nature, and impossible as it is to further it by the aid of man. No; neither cross-breeding, nor food, nor climate, we may rest assured, has the least influence in changing a green bird into a white, a brown into a yellow, or a chesnut to a grey, any more than it has in changing spots into stripes, or stripes into spots. As yet, man is ignorant of these mysterious changes, though in the pride of his intellect he would fain ascribe a reason for all he sees. This, however, seems to be beyond his reach; such knowledge is too high for him; he cannot attain unto it; beyond the fact that so many different varieties exist he positively knows nothing. It is a sealed page in the book of nature, which he cannot decipher or interpret. To those, therefore, who would fain be wise above what is written, we would say " Stand still, and consider the wondrous works of God." Yes, we would ask all such in the sublime language of Holy Writ—" Who is this that darkeneth counsel by words without knowledge? Gavest thou the goodly wings unto the peacocks? or wings and feathers unto the ostrich? Doth the hawk fly by thy wisdom, and stretch her wings toward the south? Doth the eagle mount up at thy command, and make her nest on high?"

CHAPTER X.

PRINCE CHARMING AND HIS CHARMING PRINCESS.

EBRUARY had now arrived, and with it came a few warm sunshiny days which soon had a visible effect upon our birds, and told us that the sooner we got our full complement together the better. Instead of making them more happy and peacefully inclined, it seemed to stir up all the wildest passions of their nature, as it were, in a moment, so that they were now perpetually quarrelling and fighting with each other. This told us that we must not only separate those birds which we wished to pair with each other, but also that it would soon become positively dangerous to introduce a new member into their society. To do so would be to expose him not merely to the loss of the best part of his wardrobe, but probably of his life; for when the pairing mania once begins, the canary becomes as pugnacious and savage as any of the feathered tribe. To avoid this risk, all birds that are intended to live together should be introduced not later than the first or second week in February, when usually the first symptoms of spring begin to appear. Up to this time our own birds had lived together in the most peaceful harmony possible, but two or three days of warm sunshine which occurred, as we have said, about this date, had the effect of converting the whole establishment into a scene of unceasing uproar and confusion. We had still to find, however, another pair and a half to make up what we had decided should be the full complement of our number. What kind or variety these should be we had not positively determined, but left it an open question to be decided by the chance and circumstance of the hour. One day I saw in the shop one of the richest and deepest orange-coloured birds I ever looked upon, and Mr. M— strongly recommended me to buy him. I hesitated, however, about the price, which was ten shillings, not because I thought the bird too dear, but because I wished to spend as little more money over them as I could. We thought over the matter for a day or two, when we finally decided to stretch a point for the occasion, and for this purpose Judy and I went down that day to buy him. Alas! we had driven the matter off too long, for just as we had entered the shop, Mr. M— was tying up the very bird we had come to purchase, in a parcel for another purchaser who had just bought him. We were much disappointed, and very vexed at our own delay, but it was of no use, the bird was actually sold. He was of the Belgian breed, and though not possessing very great development of shoulder, or points for a fancier's eye, yet one of the most beautiful and elegant birds I ever saw. In colour, he was a deep orange, not the least inclining to yellow, but quite red, whilst his feathers were of that silky flossy texture which, when met with in full perfection, is the climax of beauty. In so saying, however, I would not be understood as advocating the choice of a weak-feathered bird, or as depreciating the hard and close-feathered kind, which, as a general rule, I think are to be preferred. The latter are much more easily obtained, and got into fine feather than the former; but if you can get a bird whose plumage is this flossy texture and not broken, or thin and weak, but lying on it like a heavy piece of wool, and of the colour I have described above, we think you should not neglect the opportunity of purchasing if you wish to have a beautiful canary; at all events, we sorely repented neglecting the chance we had, and have never seen another since at all to equal him in the richness of his colour.

Weeks passed away without seeing anything that particularly attracted our notice, or incited our inclination to purchase, when at length Mr. M— bought a large lot of birds of a breeder in Yorkshire, and amongst them a bird very nearly resembling the one we have just described. Indeed, with the exception that he was not quite so deep in his colour, he was all that we could desire. Though of the Belgian breed, and very beautiful, he was not what would be called a fancier's bird, having no great development in that indispensable point, the shoulder. Still, take him for all in all, with the exception of the bird just mentioned, I think he is as handsome a canary as I ever saw in my life. Full seven inches in length, he has the appearance and drooping shape of a peacock when at rest, the curving outlines of his body being of the most elegant and tapering form; with a head like a snake and an eye like a hawk, he bears himself proudly amongst his fellows, over whom he exercises a lordly sway, showing unmistakably the high nobility of his birth. Of a pure rich golden yellow, at times deepening into orange, and wearing a long beautifully got-up curly shirt frill all down his breast, he stands out unrivalled and conspicuous amongst all the rest for both elegance of form and beauty of colour. We bestowed on him, as was most due, the honorable and appropriate title of " Prince Charming," a name as appropriate as it is deserved, for a very charming fellow I assure my readers he is. At the same time, we procured for him a fitting spouse, in the person of a high-bred, elegant little lady, who accordingly assumed the title of " The Charming Princess," whom he almost immediately espoused, and with whom he has ever since lived on the most affectionate and loving terms. We hope their union may be blessed by as large and numerous and as happy a family as that of our beloved queen, and that the young princes and princesses which may spring from Prince Charming and his charming princess may not only do credit to their parents, but hand down the race another generation with increasing beauty and honour to themselves.

We had now only one bird without a mate, viz., our old original maiden lady purchased to replace the one that died first given to Judy by her granny. She had been so long unwedded, and seemed so little disposed to change her state of single blessedness, that we had well nigh left her to her fate. Indeed, she was generally considered as a confirmed spinster, and seemed rather to pride herself in keeping aloof from all intercourse with any of the gentlemen of her race. In fact, if any of the latter through politeness offered her a hemp seed, or other little delicate attention, she either pointedly resented their advances, or sullenly took herself off to another quarter of the cage, evidently affronted at their presumption. With the Lizards, the Yorkshire, the London, or the cinnamon birds she would not associate at all, and was always, whilst in their company, mopish and dull. But taking her away from these, and placing her in company with the Belgian and Belgian-bred birds, she all at once became visibly more lively and sociable, so that I thought it a pity so much loveliness should be " born to blush unseen, and waste its fragrance on the desert air."

Observing this peculiarity in her disposition, and remembering how the proverb said that " birds of a feather always flock together," I at once got a clue to guide me in the choice of her mate. She was evidently of Belgian extraction herself, so I determined at once to buy the first mealy coloured, or, as they are called by fanciers, buff Belgian cock that I liked for her lord. This we soon afterwards accomplished at Mr. M—'s, making up eight pairs of very different and beautiful birds. Our last purchase proved a charming bird, of very amiable disposition and sociable manners, taking seed from our hand, and repaying us with a flood of song, drooping his wings the while like some angelic spirit about to soar aloft to heaven. Very beautiful is it to see his quivering pinions bending in a graceful curving arch towards his breast, as dancing with delight he greets you with a passionate address, and

' Shakes out of his little throat floods of delicious music."

Being of an aristocratic order we gave him at once the title of "The Marquis," and without any further ceremony introduced him to his future bride. Fortunately, the lady proved not insensible to his charms, but after a short bashfulness necessary to the occasion, accepted him as a favoured lover. The courtship was soon completed, and the lovely Dickey consented to change her name to " Daisy," and so cheated those who had looked upon her as the single old maid of the family. Great was the rejoicing on the occasion of the wedding which thus relieved the lady from a somewhat unenviable position, and at the same time secured to the gentleman an amount of domestic bliss and comfort which poor bachelors cannot possibly have the faintest idea of. The change was highly beneficial to both parties ; Daisy became as happy and sprightly as the best, though she had long been dull and mopish as one deserted and forlorn, whilst the Marquis was the gayest of the gay. As we do not suppose any are old maids from choice, for the benefit of the bachelors we will only sing the praises of a thrifty wife, and advise all such to get one as soon as they possibly can.

> "I am a cheerful fellow, altho' a married man,
> And in this age of folly pursue a saving plan :
> Though wives are thought expensive, yet who can live alone ?
> Then since they are *Dear* creatures, 'tis best to have but one.
> My choice discovers clearly my prudence and my taste,
> I've a very little wife, with a very little waste.

> "Marriage is a draught we take for better or for worse,
> And wise is he who can prevent the drafts upon his purse ;
> But evils are much lessened when wives are well inclined ;
> For if they come across us, they *shape* them to our mind :

When matters are well managed, no need to be strait-laced,
You may with little danger increase the little waste.

" Tho' Spousy's so discreet, still each fashion she'll display,
    Her bosom, Heaven bless her ! is open as the day ;
    Her garment (may I venture a simile to beg ?)
    Hangs loosely from her shoulder like a gown upon a peg ;
    Yet fearful of expenses, she shortens them so small—
    And if she goes on shortening, there'll be no waste at all."

CHAPTER XI.

OUR TURNCRESTS.

HERE is yet another variety of our favorite songster which I must not omit to mention, or which, perhaps, more correctly speaking, may be found as it were by accident in most or all the kinds we have named, to wit, the Turncrest. With some people these are great favorites, more especially with the lower classes of bird fanciers from whom anything curious or novel appears to possess a great charm. Their peculiarity consists in having a crest of feathers on the top of the head turned, as it were, the wrong way, and hanging down over the beak and eyes, something like an old-fashioned wool mop, or, if the association be not too irreverent, like the crop of a Cistercian monk. In general, as might be expected from the above remarks, they will be found most plentiful amongst the common low-bred birds of the country districts, and associated with the greatest amount of ugliness in the outline of their figure. To any one with a cultivated taste or with a natural eye for beauty of form, this condemns them at once; but in proportion as you can find this elegant appendage in birds of more aristocratic breed, such as in the Belgians; of course, this objection loses its point, and you will have a bird of peculiar elegance and beauty. Such an one

was our own King Pepin whose portrait we have given at the head of this chapter. Of gigantic stature and Herculean proportion of limb, he united singular excellence in the gracefulness of his contour, with great richness of colour. But such birds are by no means common, few having so great a degree of Belgian blood in their veins, which can alone give the snake-like head, long neck, and taper form of body peculiar to them alone. The majority we fear will be found to possess the worst properties of the commonest English birds, and, therefore, by no means to be considered an acquisition. On the contrary, if all such were to be exterminated by act of parliament, or a canary jockey club, or any other power to-morrow, we hold it would be one of the greatest boons that could possibly be conferred on the canary-loving community. We might then start afresh with birds of superior form, and breed only from those who united in themselves elegance of form with beauty of colour, when in a few years we doubt not the canary of England would be as superior to those of all other lands, as the English horse has been made to excel every other in the known world. This may seem utopian, but it is not so. It is only from ignorance and the business of breeders being left for the most part in the hands of some of the most uncultivated taste, that the present multitude of ill-shaped ugly birds that are everywhere to be seen have come into being. Let any one once see a high bred Belgian bird, and note the elegance of his shape, and then contrast it with the stumpy English specimens he has hitherto been breeding, and we will answer for it he will never be satisfied again with the latter. To the great mass of people, however, the former is a bird still unknown ; but we trust now ·that the show at Sydenham is an established reality, his excellences will soon become more widely known, and his breed be sought after to improve our own. Associated with this breed, the Turncrest will then be indeed a beautiful acquisition, as may be seen from the portrait of our own King Pepin, and to be desired will then need only to be seen.

In breeding birds of this description, most people in order to obtain the greatest development of crest pos- sible, would naturally select a male and female remark- able for the size and shape of this elegant appendage, and expect to see their offspring still more highly fa- voured in this respect than themselves.   But experience teaches otherwise, and emphatically says that if we do thus, the result will in all probability be in diametrical opposition to our wishes.   All writers, and every breeder I have spoken to upon the subject, unanimously declare that if we pair two crested birds together, the majority of their offspring, so far from being more highly favoured than their parents, will absolutely be more or less de- ficient in this appendage so much desired, if their heads are not positively bald! Why this should be the case I cannot tell, nor could I ever obtain any satisfactory explanation of the matter, or, indeed, any reason at all beyond that it is so, which, therefore, I must beg my readers to take as conclusive upon the subject, adding that I myself have never personally put the matter to the test, which, however, after the assurances I have received from practical men, I should be sorry to doubt.

To obtain birds with fine crests, the practice is to select one parent only with this appendage, which signifies little, though for my part I should prefer it to be the hen, as we know from many careful experiments that have been made, that it is the male that contributes for the most part the bones and what may be termed the locomotive organs, and the female the internal organs on which depend the skin, and, consequently, the feathers, which, of course, form the crest. As in the human being, experience often shows that minds formed of the most opposite attributes more forcibly attract each other than those which appear cast in the same mould, so we suppose a similar effect is produced in the bodily organism of our pets, and that in the case of our turncrests the rule of contraries is more potent than the rule of harmonies. The greater the contrast the greater the fascination, and the more likelihood of success. In this respect, extremes shall meet, and a beauteous offspring of crested birds shall spring from a crested cock and smooth-headed hen, or from a crested hen and smooth-headed cock, which reminds me of that striking contrast drawn by an anonymous poet between man and woman in the following very beautiful lines :

> " Man is the rugged, lofty pine,
>   That frowns on many a wave-beat shore ;
> Woman, the slender, graceful vine,
> Whose circling tendrils round it twine,
>   And deck its rough bark sweetly o'er.

> " Man is the rock whose towering crest
>   Nods o'er the mountain's barren side ;
> Woman, the soft and mossy nest
> That loves to clasp the sterile breast,
>   And wreathe its brow in verdant pride.

" Man is the cloud of coming storm,
 Dark as the raven's murky plume,
Save where the sunbeam, light and warm,
Of woman's soul and woman's form,
 Beams brightly o'er the gathering gloom.

" Yes, lovely sex, to you 'tis given
 To rule our hearts with angel sway;
Blend with each woe a blissful leaven—
Change earth into an embryo heaven—
 And sweetly smile our cares away."

CHAPTER XII.

THE DOMINIE AND THE GERMANS.

E had now completed our stock of canaries for breeding, having eight pairs, four for each compartment of our aviary. We had thus specimens of every kind of breed, and almost every variety of colour. Belgians with their fine orange yellow and peculiar form, lizards with their beautifully speckled plumage of grey and yellow green; the London fancy with its burnished golden body and jet black wings and tail; Yorkshire spangles with their gaily marked heads and wings; the pure grass green, the mealy white or buff, and the beautiful chesnut, fawn, or cinnamon, as they are more commonly called. We had thus far been highly successful in realising the plan we had sketched out for ourselves, and now possessed birds of almost every form and colour. To make our establishment quite complete, there was one thing still wanting, viz., an accomplished vocalist; for, though we had several very excellent singers amongst our gentlemen canaries, yet their song was only the uncultivated and inartistic ditty of England. But as the time was fast approaching when we hoped to have a numerous progeny of young princes and scions of noble blood, we felt it a duty to provide a suitable master for their vocal educa-

6

tion. As we knew we should look in vain for such among our English birds, we turned to the land of song and music, and sought what we wanted in the fatherland of Germany.

In respect of song, the German birds are as much superior to those of England, or, indeed, of any country I am acquainted with, as the high-bred Belgian is in form to the little short stumpy canary we see in every market. The reason of this is very simple. On the one hand, the Germans pay great attention, and bestow much pains on the education of these little songsters; whereas, on the other, the Englishman leaves all to chance, never troubling his head about the matter. With us a bird is left entirely to its own resources, scarcely ever hearing any other note than that of its parent, from one generation to another, so that we need scarcely be surprised to find the same piercing loud and harsh song handed down from father to son without the least change or improvement. Far different is it, however, in Germany, where the breeding of canaries is quite a trade, and which, therefore, to make it profitable, requires and receives as much attention and thought as any other. There the greatest pains are taken to teach the young birds an artificial song; and such has been their success that it has enhanced their value some twenty per cent. Indeed, were it not that they have no rivals in the matter of song, they would never be able to sell the little ordinary variety, which alone they breed, in England at all. As it is, thousands are now annually imported into our country, and find a ready sale at prices varying from ten to five and twenty shillings each, which but for their song would not make more than eighteen pence at the most. Instead of the high piercing note continued for some time by the English bird without intermission, rising higher and higher, or modified only by a succession of noisy bursts, the German begins with a low sweet trill, like the sibilating sound of the grasshopper on a summer's eve, and with a silvery sonorous voice regularly descends through all the tones of an octave, introducing from time to time a bell-like succession of notes, or the song of the woodlark and the nightingale as the case may be. So great is the difference between the two, and such is the result of careful painstaking teaching, as compared with the let-alone, give-myself-no-trouble plan adopted by English breeders.

The same writer who, as I have shown elsewhere, exhibited so much ignorance about the Belgian canary, betrays equal want of knowledge about the German, when he talks about their wholesale manufacture by simply putting English birds into little wooden cages similar to those in which the real Germans are always imported. No doubt John Bull is a very stupid creature in many things, but we fancy he is not quite such a fool as to believe such stuff as this. The writer alluded to would have us believe that there is little or no difference between an English bird and a German in the matter of song, so that a purchaser may be easily imposed upon. All that we can say is, that any one who has once heard any number of German birds sing, could not possibly be taken in, and that a man would hardly be such a fool, we think, as to buy a bird for his song without hearing him sing. No one, we will venture to say, could be possibly taken in by so silly a trick as the one thus asserted to be commonly practised by dealers. Moreover, for a man to do so systematically, even could similar cages and birds be made and obtained sufficiently cheap to make it worth the while, which I very much doubt, would most assuredly be the shortest way to ruin he could possibly devise. He might, perhaps, succeed in taking in an unwary customer once, but would any one in his senses suffer himself thus to be duped a second time? Most assuredly not; but setting this palpable fact aside, we say again the song is utterly unlike that of the English bird in every respect; once heard it can never be mistaken, even by the most unmusical ear; and to be appreciated it requires, we are sure, only to be heard. If I wanted a bird merely for its song, I would rather give a pound for a German than I would give half-a-crown for an English bird, or, indeed, have one given me for nothing. The best are said to come from the Tyrol and the Hartz, where large numbers are annually reared and sent into every part of Europe. For many years past four Tyrolese alone have been known to bring over as many as sixteen hundred birds, each in a separate little wooden cage about six inches square, in which he has to travel more than one thousand miles, and live till he is sold to some purchaser in a dealer's shop in England. The trade increases steadily almost every year, as their song is appreciated by the English public, and their price maintains its position in the market, for almost every proprietor of a gin-palace finds it to his interest to have one or two in his place, so great is their attraction in the eyes of the people who are thus privileged to hear them sing.

Observing that Seraph, whom we purchased from a German dealer, had, though full-grown, acquired in a very short time the song of the German birds with whom he had been only accidentally associated, I felt persuaded that we had only to get a good songster from the fatherland, and to place our young birds under his tuition, and they would soon be as proficient as their teacher. I determined, therefore, to get one the first opportunity I might have, and at all events make the experiment. For this we had not long to wait, as about the end of February, Mr. M— set off for the continent and brought back a large number of Germans, amongst which were some excellent songsters. As I entered the shop, one gush of melody burst upon my enraptured ear, each bird striving to outdo its neighbour in the length and beauty of its song. It seemed, indeed, like the rippling of a thousand streams murmuring in silvery and liquid tones over some pebbly bed, so exquisitely soft and incessant was the strain. But how amongst so many shall we even attempt to make a choice? Amongst so much excellence how are we to proceed? Surely it must be to a great extent a matter of chance whether we get the bird whose song we like most to hear. One bird may be better than another for its melody or its looks, or *vice versâ*, as the case may be—how amongst so many obtain the one most to our liking? Well, there is no chance in the matter, the nature and quality of each bird's song is accurately known. Each bird has a separate number marked on his cage, which is duly registered in a book, which thus indicates the name of the breeder, the particular character of the song all his birds are taught, which again is chequed by the private mark of the dealer or dealers through whose hand he has passed. You have, therefore, only to separate one or two birds at a time, and take them into another room by themselves and hear them sing, and make your choice between the various songs you may hear. Having done this, you may then select from all the birds bearing this number the one whose appearance you like best, and you will obtain without much difficulty the bird you most desire. All bred by one breeder have the same song, and one is better than another only in the accidents of the quality of his voice, the pleasing appearance of his looks or the soundness of his constitution. Most of them are very plain-looking birds, being mealy in their colour, and very short and stumpy in their figure. They are, therefore, very small and inelegant, to use only a mild term, compared with either the Belgian or the more highly-bred birds among the English. "Handsome, however, is he that handsome does," assuredly applies to the little German from the Tyrol or the Hartz, and for a parlour companion he easily bears away the bell. Some talk about his being more delicate than the English, and requiring much more care and attention to keep him in full song. My own experience proves the contrary. My own bird is as hardy, if not the hardiest, of any canary that we have, though kept in a small cage by himself, instead of having a roomy aviary for exercise. Moreover, his food has been of the simplest and most ordinary kind, viz., common canary seed mixed with a little rape, with now and then a few hemp for a relish, or a bit of apple or lettuce as the season may be, and a bit of sopped toast every morning as we sit down to breakfast. He has never been either sick or sorry, not even whilst moulting, whilst his song is almost incessant all day long, singing even at night by candle-light, waking up even at midnight for the purpose whenever he is placed upon the table. I cannot, therefore, believe that they are at all more delicate or difficult to keep than any other, but that where ordinary care and attention, in the matter of proper food and temperature are bestowed upon them, they will be found as hardy as any of our English, and much more hardy than the Belgian varieties we have yet met with.

As I intended ours to be a parlour bird, I naturally desired to unite beauty of appearance and excellence of song in the same bird. In this I happily succeeded, choosing a very sprightly, strong-looking little bird, prettily marked on the head and back, with rich chesnut brown, who happened to be an excellent singer as well. Highly pleased with my bargain I hasten to transport him home, when he immediately treated us to a song. The success of his first *debut* was complete! all who heard him were enraptured with his performance, and pronounced him to be truly a master in his art. He thus graduated in high honours as a Doctor of Music, and was at once elected as professor and tutor to the young princes and nobles in our aviary. The office conferred upon him as well a name which he continues to maintain with the dignity due to his position. Without more to-do, then, let me introduce to my readers, the now famous and much-admired " Dominie."

"Much did I grieve, on that ill-fated morn,
  When I was first to school reluctant borne;
  Severe I thought the dame, though oft she tried
  To soothe my swelling spirits when I sighed:
  And oft, when harshly she reproved, I wept,
  To my lone corner, broken-hearted crept,
  And thought of tender home, where anger never kept.

"But soon inured to alphabetic toils,
  Alert I met the dame with jocund smiles;
  First at the form, my task for ever true,
  A little favorite rapidly I grew;
  And oft she stroked my head with fond delight,
  Held me a pattern to the dunce's sight,
  And, as she gave my diligence its praise,
  Talked of the honours of my future days."

CHAPTER XIII.

ON MULES.

FOR some people anything that is incongruous or grotesque, or that in any way is a departure from the ordinary laws of nature, appears to possess a peculiar charm. This is more especially observable in the less educated classes of society, who delight in the monsters usually exhibited at country fairs, and for whom what may be termed a freak of nature has a hundred times more attraction than the most perfect form, or the greatest combination of excellence and quality. Nor is this so much to be wondered at, for to appreciate the latter qualities implies a mind educated to admire, and able to compare and weigh whatever is superior to the common standard, whereas to admire the former requires only the stupid gaze of astonishment and wonder. Hence the rage among such people for everything that is out of the ordinary track of nature, and their frequent attempts to mar her handiwork by mating birds of different species with each other. A mule or hybrid for them has a charm and value far beyond the most perfect specimen of a true bred bird, though neither in colour, shape, or song can it possibly have the least claim to be compared. With such tastes and feelings it is needless to say we have little sympathy; still, as some of my readers, by no means open to the charge implied in the above remarks, may desire to make a few experiments for themselves, we will say a few words upon the most desirable birds to begin with, and the results most likely to be attained.

According to Bechstein, the species which succeed best with the canary are the serin, the citril, the siskin, the goldfinch, and the linnet. The greenfinch, the chaffinch, the bullfinch, and yellowhammer, he adds, have been tried, but the difficulty augments with the difference of species and food ; for example I have never seen a male canary very fond of a female yellow-hammer, nor a male of the latter kind of a female canary, though the plumage may be selected so as to offer a striking resemblance. An ardent bullfinch will sometimes yield to the allurements of a very ardent hen canary. I have myself witnessed it; but with every care it is seldom the eggs are very fruitful, and produce young. Dr. Jassy, however, writes me from Frankfort that he has obtained mules of a bullfinch and canary, by making other canaries sit on the eggs, and bring up the young, and that this plan is pursued in Bohemia. My bullfinch, he adds, is so attached to the female canary that he mourns all the time they are separated, and cannot bear any other bird.

Although Bechstein enumerates the yellow-hammer as a mate for the canary in the list given above, we ourselves can amply bear out the qualifying remark he makes as to the unlikelihood of a match—as we have repeatedly made the experiment with birds between whom there was very little difference of colour, and always with the like result. Although this, at first sight may seem somewhat strange, it is readily accounted for when we remember that the yellowhammer is not a finch, but a bunting, and consequently that the two birds belong to two different species which have little or no affinity with each other.

The same remark holds good also with regard to the greenfinch, which together with its congener, the bull-finch, although commonly called finches, do not belong to the finch tribe, but are members of the gros-beak species, which we think is sufficient to put it also out of the category of desirable or likely mates for the canary.

The serin, the citril, and the siskin, not being common in England, we can say little about, never having tried the two former, whilst we have possessed two of the latter, neither of which ever showed the least signs of mating with any of our canaries, with whom they were constantly kept. That others have been more successful we do not doubt, but we think we may safely say that the chance of success with all these is at the best but indifferent and remote. A mule between a canary and a citril finch, if the former is neither white nor yellow, says Bechstein, differs little from the common grey or green canary, except in being more slender, and having the beak shorter and thicker; while a mule between a siskin and canary, if the mother be a green canary, will resemble a female siskin; but if she be white or yellow their colours are lighter, yet without differing greatly from those of the siskin, which they always resemble in shape.

We come then at last to the three English finches, viz., the chaffinch, the linnet, and the goldfinch, as being the most likely of any to ensure success, and as being perhaps the most desirable when obtained. Singularly enough, however, common as the chaffinch is amongst our gardens and orchards we have never met with one that has ever been paired with a canary, and never heard of such a thing as a hybrid produced from them in this country. Here, however, they are not held in the same esteem as in Germany, where, such is the passion for these birds, that men have been known to travel ninety miles from home to take with bird-lime one of these birds, distinguished for its song, and have given one of their cows for a fine songster having what is termed the double trill of the Hartz. We cannot enter into all the niceties of the chaffinch's song, and beautiful as his plumage undoubtedly is when flitting about in our orchards and gardens, it soon loses its freshness and colour in confinement, and hence in England it is little prized and seldom kept, and thus it too may be dismissed as not affording much prospect of success.

Our choice, then, seems to lie principally between the linnet and the goldfinch, both of which are easily paired with the canary, and from both of which mules are with little difficulty obtained. The offspring of both these mixtures combine more or less the colours of the parents, and participate in the shape of the male linnet or goldfinch, rather than that of the female canary. We need scarcely say, therefore, that the produce of the linnet will always present a heavy

stumpy appearance, and consequently be more or less
unsightly to the eye that has any perception of beauty
of outline, while that of the goldfinch will necessarily
have more gracefulness of figure, and a greater variety
of plumage.   The colour of the former will be the
brown of the linnet, perhaps blotched with patches of
dingy white, while that of the latter will partake more
of the gay livery of the goldfinch with a far greater
diversity in its plumage.   We ourselves have bred
specimens some of which differed little from the male
goldfinch, while others have united the beautiful scarlet
and orange head of the former, with a body of beautiful
and delicate white like a canary.   We have seen others
of most exquisite shape, and most attractive colour,
from which, although no admirers of the mule tribe in
general, it were impossible to withhold our meed of praise.
" The most beautiful I have seen," says Bechstein,
" was greyish ash-colour in the middle of its crest, and
silvery white on the rest of its head and nape ; a broad
orange border surrounded the beak, and the neck was
adorned with a white collar ; the back was dusky grey
with black streaks ; the rump white, the under part of
the body of a snowy whiteness ; the under tail-coverts
the wings, and first quill-feathers white, but the others
as well as the coverts, black edged with yellow ; the
middle of the wing was also adorned with a beautiful
golden yellow spot ; the white tail had a black spot on
the sides ; the white beak was tipped with black ; the
feet were white.   The mother of this beautiful bird
was white with a greenish-grey crest.   In general one
may be sure of fine birds when yellow or white females

are paired with male goldfinches. The song of both the linnet and goldfinch mule is sufficiently pleasing and attractive, while that of all others may be said to be the reverse, which again is a great recommendation in their favour. After all, however, we think the trouble and risk of disappointment are scarcely worth running for the chance of a prize bird, which, like angels' visits, is certain to be few and far between. For one handsome bird you may safely reckon on a dozen ill-favoured, if not positively ugly. In any case if any one wishes to make the experiment, he must remember that whether he select the serin, the citril, the siskin, yellowhammer, greenfinch, bullfinch, chaffinch, linnet, or goldfinch, to ensure success, the female must always be a canary, and that these must not be old birds caught by the birdcatcher as chance may direct, but be brought up from the nest by hand; otherwise disappointment and failure will be almost certain to result. As an occasional experiment the attempt to obtain birds of this kind will have its charms and attractions for many, but for ourselves we confess we care little for mules in any shape or form. A wise Providence has set the mark of sterility on all such heterogenous offspring, and while it has thus said, as though in displeasure at the attempt to transgress its laws, "Hitherto shalt thou go, and no farther," on the other hand, we read on the first page of Holy Writ how, when God commanded the water to bring forth abundantly every living creature that moveth, and every winged fowl, each was to be "after his kind." In this way alone He bestowed His blessing upon them and commanded them thus to replenish the earth. "What God hath joined together let no man put asunder," and what he hath put asunder let no man attempt to bring together.

"God spake : the waters teem with life,
     The tenants of the floods ;
  The many-coloured wingèd birds
    Dart quickly through the woods.
       High rushes the eagle,
         On fiery wings ;
       Low hid in the valley,
         The nightingale sings.

"God spake : the lion, steer, and horse,
     Spring from the moistened clay,
  While round the breast of mother earth
    Bees hum, and lambkins play.
       They give life to the mountain,
         They swarm on the plain,
       But their eyes fix'd on earth,
         Must for ever remain.

"God spake: He look'd on earth and heaven,
     With mild and gracious eye :
  In His own image man He made,
    And gave Him dignity.
       He springs from the dust,
         The Lord of the earth,
       The chorus of heaven,
         Exult at his birth.
       And now creation's work was ended,
         Man raised his head, he spoke ;
       The day of rest by God ordain'd,
         The sabbath morning broke."

CHAPTER XIV.

PREPARATIONS FOR BREEDING, TIME, MANNER, AND
OBJECT OF PAIRING.

HAVING thus completed our stock of birds, the time was now at hand for their proper assortment. Notwithstanding the popular rural tradition that on St. Valentine's Day each bird of the air chooses its mate, and that we had the express license of old Chaucer to put up the banns of union on so auspicious a day, we decline to begin so early. Though as anxious as any one to commence these important preliminaries, and though the weather just then happened to be peculiarly favorable and tempting, we thought it better to wait a little longer, for fear we might find to our cost that in the more haste there is often the worst speed. In vain did the oldest of our English poets proclaim his mandate in our ears, saying,

> " Foules take heed of my sentence, I pray,
>   And for your own ease in fordring of your need,
>   As fast as I may speak, I will me speed :
> Ye know well how, on St. Valentine's day,
>   By my statute, and through my governaunce,
> Ye do chuse your mates, and after flie away
>   With him, as I move you with plesaunce."

We do not believe anything is to be gained by commencing operations so early, for even should a person

succeed in getting young birds hatched by the beginning or middle of March, they are invariably delicate
and tender, and difficult to rear.   Moreover, should the
weather change and become cold and frosty, as it not
unfrequently does about this time, not only are the
young birds almost sure to perish from want of the
necessary warmth of the sun, but the old birds are
unduly weakened by their exertions, and much loss of
time and disappointment are the result.   In the choice
of time for pairing young birds, much, of course, must
depend upon circumstances.   If the weather is very
fine and your birds strong and in good condition, the
latter end of March or beginning of April may be selected if you are very anxious to begin ; but as a general
rule if you wait till the middle of the latter month, it
will be quite early enough.   Young birds require great
warmth, and, it must be remembered, warmth of the sun,
too, in order to develop their feathers properly, which
fact alone, if borne in mind, will tell you when is the
most proper time to begin.   Any how, we may dismiss
the popular tradition of St. Valentine's day as a popular
fallacy, more honoured in the breach than in the ob-
servance.   It may be all very well for poets to sing
about this festive day, and explicitly declare, as Iago
does, how thereon

> " The tuneful choir, in amorous strains,
>   Accost their feathered loves ;
>   While each fond mate, with equal pains,
>   The tender suit approves."

but it will scarcely do for practical men in this matter-
of-fact age, to heed their strain.   In such a case, I

7

would rather give the somewhat unpalatable advice which Crabbe has given on a similar occasion, and say,

> " Disposed to wed, e'en while you hasten, stay,—
> There's great advantage in a small delay."

In order to bring about a match as we desired, for our birds were all together, a little manœuvring and management became necessary, or our plan of operations would very probably have been marred. The manner of bringing this about we accomplished in the following way, which, as it proved both simple and effective, I would recommend to others. Having fixed upon the birds we wished to pair together, we separated them from the rest, placing them by themselves in two different cages in another room. For a couple of days we hung one bird above the other, in such a manner as the one could only just get a glimpse of his neighbour. This excited their curiosity, and caused them to begin to call to each other, and at the same time made them more desirous than they would otherwise have been, to form an acquaintance with their unknown friend. Very droll it was to watch their manœuvres to accomplish this desirable object, and try to overcome every difficulty in the way. While the lady below clung to the sides and roof of her cage, the gentleman above stretched out its neck to its utmost length, if perchance he might obtain a glimpse of her charming person. To obtain a more perfect sight of his intended bride, the latter would now descend to the floor of his cage, and walk on tip-toe, looking with the intensest gaze over its ledge, and now mount to the topmost wires of the roof, which, alas ! improved his position but little. Then he would

drop down to his ordinary perch and serenade her with
a song, recounting, no doubt, in enraptured strains all
the charming qualities of her person and the intolerable
sorrows of his state.   Then she would answer with a
chirp, as though she would assure him she had no objection to his suit, when again he would go his rounds
as before.   The third day, knowing how " hope de-
ferred maketh the heart sick," and that it will not do
to trifle with the affections thereof too long, we placed
the two cages side by side, when for several hours they
were permitted to enjoy a cozy *tête-à-tête* through the
wires.   Loth to lose so golden an opportunity, the gentleman, feeling that " a faint heart never wins a fair
lady," soon popped the question to his mistress, who
in reply twittered out a bashful assent to his suit, when
a low sweet warbling declared the engagement complete.   The doors were then opened ; he hopped into
her apartment, and she accompanied him back to his,
when having seen all that there was to be seen, and
partaken of the daintiest morsels of his larder, they
retire to bill and coo together at their leisure, till their
happiness is complete.   Substituting the cage and aviary
for the meadow and the spray, we may apply the lines
of the poet to their case.

> " With cheerful hop from spray to spray,
>   They sport along the meads,
>   In social bliss together stray
>   Where love or fancy leads.
>
>   Through spring's gay scenes each happy pair
>   Their fluttering joys pursue ;
>   Its various charms and produce share,
>   For ever kind and true."

Having thus spoken of the time and manner of pairing, we would now say a word upon the object to be kept in view. With many persons a canary is a canary, and so that young birds are produced they care not what they are; but this plan, if such it can be called, not only necessarily prevents the attainment of excellence, but destroys, we think, half the interest and enjoyment of the occupation. In breeding canaries, as in all other things, the axiom of Dr. Johnson, " that whatever is worth doing at all is worth doing well," should ever be borne in mind. Were it only acted upon, we should not see the number of common little, ugly marked, ill-shaped birds we do, but all would be more or less like the prize birds, larger in size, elegant in shape, and rich and regular in colour. Although, as in the case of cattle in the agricultural world, prizes and exhibitions in London and other large towns have done much to improve the breed of our canaries, yet the progress is slow; and I fear it will still be many years before their influence is generally felt, and the race of misshapen and irregular blotched birds are extirpated from our land.

To every breeder, therefore, of this pretty songster, I would say, start out with some definite object in your own mind, and then having settled what this shall be, devote all the skill and knowledge you possess to bring it about. For example, study the varieties of *form* peculiar to each race, settle in your own mind a high standard of elegance, and then select those birds alone to breed from you think are most likely to realise it in their produce. Do the same as to *colour*, decide at the outset what this shall be, and do all you can to get it pure and distinct. Thus, whether it be pure white, pale lemon, or buff, bright yellow, or deep orange, grey or green, cinnamon or mottled ; in short, whether it be the Lizard, the London fancy, or the Yorkshire spangle, or prize Belgian, do not miss them but keep them separate, selecting such birds only as are likely in your judgment to produce offspring still more excellent than their parents. This, you may rest assured, will not only be the most likely way of improving the breed to which your special attention may chance to be directed, but will impart an additional interest to the undertaking, which mere chance or promiscuous breeding would fail to yield. In our own case, excellence in colour, and elegance of shape, song being for the most part a matter of after education, were the two points we specially aimed at. With regard to shape, there is little or no difficulty to contend with, the rule of " like producing like" invariably holding good. With regard to colour, however, owing I imagine to the promiscuous breeding and crossing hitherto practised, it is nothing like so certain. Could you only obtain birds of any given colour, whose ancestors had never been crossed with those of any other for eight or ten generations previously, I have little doubt but that it would be as constant and unchanging as any other quality you could name. But owing to the want of the systematic breeding we recommend, this rule can hardly be depended upon at present, or, indeed, any other, for all are liable to be marred by vagaries which the breeder could not possibly anticipate. Hence also the discrepancies and

conflicting advice given by various writers upon the
subject, such being true probably as regards his own
unlimited experience, but scarcely to be relied on as an
unalterable rule for all. Thus, one writer whom we
have consulted lays down the law clearly and tersely:
" If you wish very high-coloured birds, breed jonque
and jonque," that is, bright yellow with bright yellow,
whilst another as confidently asserts that such a mode
of proceeding will never do, but that "a fine full-
coloured yellow bird is most likely to be obtained from
the union of a clear-bred jonque cock with a large perfect mealy hen." Who shall decide when doctors dis-
agree? As in the matter of medicine, the homœopaths
and the allopaths are diametrically opposed in the prin-
ciples on which their practice is based, the one asserting
that like cures like, and the other clinging as strictly
to the contraries, so do authors who treat upon the
breeding of the canary. One party asserts without
fear of contradiction, " that the union of opposites are
productive of the most harmonious results," the other
that their experience teaches the very contrary. For
my own part, I believe much depends upon the particular circumstances of each case. Wherever we can
obtain pure bred birds from a pure stock of several generations I have no doubt about the soundness and
wisdom of the homœopathic principle of " like producing
like." But where birds have been cross bred with others
of different colour, or where it is desirable to infuse a
harder texture into the soft and flossy silkiness of
feather usually found in very high-coloured birds, a
cross with a close-feathered mealy hen may be more

desirable. As an instance of the rule of contraries, it is universally admitted that two mop-headed, or turned-down-crested birds, will produce bald-pated offspring. Why, I believe, is not understood. Of the truth of this I cannot personally speak of my own knowledge, never having made the experiment. However, whilst adhering to the maxim of like producing like, it is only fair to state the caution I received from the German importer when I bought my green hen to match with a cock of similar colour. " You do tink," said my informant in quaint and broken English, " you do tink to have green birds by pairing dis green hen with a cock like her." " Certainly," I replied. " Well, me do tink no such ting; me tink you will have clear yellow ones." " Well," I rejoined, " we shall see; at all events I will try and make the experiment, for, after all, there is nothing like personal experience in such matters." Though I have not succeeded in rearing any from the birds in question, yet we succeeded in having several young birds hatched and reared until they had fine feathers on their back, all of which were exceedingly dark, and showed no approach to anything like yellow. Mr. Adams in his ' Cage and Singing Birds,' says good Lizards are obtained by matching a strongly marked grey cock with a dark-splashed hen, and if you put together a strong grey or green-coloured cock with a clear mealy hen, you will most likely have what are called cinnamon birds; the lightest tinted of this variety are termed quakers; and if you match a quaker hen with a clear greenish cock, you get what is called the dove canary, from the soft, subdued colour of its plumage. If you pair for several seasons the lightest mealies procurable, you will have white and flaxen-coloured birds, and so you may go on producing varieties innumerable. For our own part, however, we recommend the system of like producing like, keeping these clear and distinct, rather than crossing and re-crossing as above described; but, above all, the breeding of self-coloured birds rather than of irregularly or fancifully marked birds we now too often see.

> " Rejoice, my merry little mate,
>   The blithesome spring is coming,
> When thou shalt roam, with heart elate,
>   To hear the wild bee humming;
> To hear the wild bee humming round
>   The primrose sweetly blowing,
> And listen to each gentle sound
>   Of gladsome music flowing.
>
> " The birds shall sing from many a bower,
>   Joy like thy own obeying;
> And round full many a blooming flower
>   The butterfly be playing—
> Be playing, love, on wings as light
>   As heart in thy young bosom,
> And showing tints as fair and bright
>   As does the opening blossom.
>
> " The snowdrops by our garden walk
>   Long since to life have started—
> They wither now upon the stalk;
>   Their beauty is departed—
> Their beauty is departed.   But
>   Flowers in the fields are springing,
> Which by and bye shall ope and shut,
>   As to the glad birds singing.

*   *   *   *

" Spring is to me no happy time,
 Its smiles are touch'd with sadness ;
For vanish'd, with life's early prime,
 Is much that gave it gladness.
Yet, merry playmate, for thy sake,
 I will not sing of sorrow ;
But since thou canst its joys partake,
 I would 'twere spring to-morrow."

CHAPTER XV.

NEST-BOXES AND NESTS.

HAVING paired all our birds, and returned them to the aviary, the next thing that became necessary was to provide them with the means of making their nest. When wild the canary, as we have already stated, loves to build its nest in the branches of the orange-tree on the banks of some silver stream, where the perfume of the flowers seems most grateful to its taste. To gratify this very natural propensity of their nature was wholly out of our power, we having neither orange-trees nor greenhouse to offer them. Use, however, we knew was second nature, and therefore as the latter is proverbially accommodating to the circumstances in which it finds itself, we did not despair of inducing our feathered friends to put up with a much more humble and unromantic situation. Their locality was fixed, and from that there was no escape. If it could not be said to be quite so poetical as the banks of a stream, or the perfumed orangery of a greenhouse, still it was light, cheerful, airy, and above all of even temperature, and altogether free from cold and chilling draughts, points specially to be attended to in the breeding and keeping of the canary. Nothing is more injurious to their health than great

and sudden changes in the temperature, and nothing
kills them so soon as the exposure to a cold draught.
Too much heat is to be avoided as much as too little,
the former making the hens sickly, produces weakening
perspirations very injurious to their own health, as well
as causes their young to be weak and difficnlt to rear.
As we had no trees, or anything that could be taken as
an apology for one, two things were manifestly re
quired, viz., materials wherewith to make their nest,
and something wherein the nest might be made in.
We looked about, and saw, both in the market and in
the shop-windows of the dealers, pretty little wicker-
work baskets, a trifle larger than the panniers usually
placed on the back of a toy-jackass, with building
materials corresponding to their size. We were too
practical to be taken in with such toys, and abjured
them from the first with as much contempt as would a
true disciple of old Isaac the tempting flies and taking
gear usually found in a fashionable fishing-tackle shop
in town. In lieu thereof we had a number of wooden
boxes made, of the following proportions, viz., three
and three quarter inches long, by thiee and a quarter
wide, and two deep, in fact, common kitchen soap-
boxes, the back finishing in a point, and having a long
hole so as to take on and off a hook placed in the wall
for that purpose. These were both neat in their
appearance, and commodious for the birds, requiring
indeed a little more material to fill them, but prevent-
ing the risk of the young birds falling out of their nest,
and coming to an untimely end, at the same time that
they were easy to exchange and keep clean.

Placing one in each corner of the aviary, and others midway between, we left each bird to select his own plot of building-ground, as whim or fancy might direct. Very amusing was it to watch each newly-married couple setting off on a house-hunting expedition. With critical eye and searching glance they inspected all the ins and outs of their future domicile, weighing the advantages and drawbacks to each with discriminating wisdom and caution. One pair evidently liked to see all that was going on in the bustling and busy scene of the little world around them, and chose a handsome villa residence close to the wire fencing which formed the boundary of their domain ; another, more shy and retiring, selected a quiet cozy-looking domicile in an out-of-the-way corner at the back, into which no inquisitive passer-by might look or intrude ; a third evidently looked out for a bright and cheerful aspect, having an eye to the early rays of the morning sun ; while a fourth, reflecting how all their domestic comfort might be destroyed, could every idle, gossiping neighbour overlook their house, selected the highest situation they could find, from whence they could look down with an air of conscious superiority on all below. In a word, some liked light, and some shade, some the activity of the world, some the retirement of the cloister, and thus it came to pass, one way or other, each selected the spot that pleased them best ; and though there was but one vase of water for each four houses, the ladies contrived to live in harmony and peace, instead of, as is too often the case under such circumstances with the human race, wasting many hard words over a little soft water, and striving hard like echo to have the last word.

Well, but after all, you will say, these wooden boxes are but the bricks and mortar of their residence, the bare walls, as it were, of their house, how did they fit them up and furnish them? In human families, most of us know, when a little stranger is expected, great preparations are made for his proper reception. There is a nice wicker cradle, a soft and downy mattress for his bed, fine warm woollen blankets to keep him warm, to say nothing of the white pincushion with its pink or blue ribbon, and customary salutation inscribed in pinny type, saying, "Welcome little stranger!" What have you then to correspond with all this? Where did you go a shopping? Who was your upholsterer and cabinet-maker, and how did you provide for their wants? Happily all these questions are soon answered; we had no suites of expensive mahogany, rosewood, or walnut, to purchase; there was no perplexity in choosing between oak and maple-painted or japan ware; we had no anxiety about either the colour of our curtains, or the texture of our carpets; lace and muslin, damask or chintz, silk or moreen, had no charms for our newly-married couples. No, they cared not a rush for Axminster or Turkey, Brussels or velvet pile, Scotch or Kidderminster, felt or drugget, cocoa-nut or oilcloth for their flooring. Having no windows they required neither venetians for their blinds, or white or buff hollands to keep out the sun. Gold cornices and rods were alike dispensed with; being always on the wing they wanted neither staircase nor other carpet in

their bedroom, or rocking-chair to lull them to sleep.
No, the furnishing of their house was a much more
simple and inexpensive a matter.   A little moss from
some old forest tree, a little hair from the cow with the
crumpled horn, and a little raw cotton given me by a
kind friend, notwithstanding half the mills in Manchester were either on the point of stopping or of
putting their hands on short time, through lack of
sufficient material to carry on their business, owing to
the mortal strife then going on between the Northern
and Southern States of America, was all that we
required.   Having first thoroughly cleaned the moss,
and scalded the hair with boiling water, for the purpose
of killing all vermin that might be therein, we dried it
again before the fire, and then with a further addition
of cotton, put the whole in little string nets made for
the purpose, which we hung outside the wires of the
aviary, that the birds might not pull it all in pieces by
way of amusement, as otherwise they would be very
likely to do.   The moss made a very good mattress,
the hair answered the purpose of a good feather bed,
whilst the cotton supplied the place of a pair of the
warmest witney blankets or eider-down quilt, shutting
out all cold, and making altogether a couch such as the
most luxurious lady of the land might envy and desire.
Unlike the English finches, to wit, the goldfinch,
chaffinch, and linnet, the canary finch is but a rough
and clumsy builder, caring comparatively little for the
external neatness of its nest, though the interior is laid
in and finished with considerable care and attention to
its appearance.   Still, of its performance, no less than of

that of these superior artists, may we say with Hurdis, in that beautiful poem entitled " The Village Curate,"

" But most of all, it wins my admiration,
  To view the structure of this little work,
  A bird's nest.   Mark it well !—within, without ;
  No tool had he that wrought—no knife to cut,
  No nail to fix—no bodkin to insert—
  No glue to join ; his little beak was all.
  And yet how neatly finished !   What nice hand,
  With every implement and means of art,
  And twenty years' apprenticeship to boot,
  Could make me such another ?   Fondly, then,
  We boast of excellence, whose noblest skill
  Instinctive genius foils."

CHAPTER XVI.

OUR FIRST BIRDS.

N the 26th of March, the weather being fine, and our birds strong, and we ourselves all anxiety and impatience to begin, we first put the nest-boxes and materials for building into the aviary. Immediately all was wonder and excitement amongst the birds. The hens bustled about from one box to another, curiously inspecting every nook and corner, each apparently afraid lest her neighbour should be first in the field. Although in taking a house many inquiries have to be made, which little girls who live at home at ease, and which bachelors and spinsters domiciling in lodgings ready for their use have little conception of, it was evident, as there were many applicants for the same tenement, they had no time to lose. Our birds seemed to be of this opinion, and as it usually happens in such cases, so it did with them. The least and most energetic little hen in the whole aviary at once decided upon the most eligible villa in the square, and forthwith took possession by lining it with moss and hair. Whilst others were looking about, unable to make up their minds, or wasting their time in picking at the hair and cotton, little Blanche had half finished her nest. Not a moment did she lose, though her lordly husband proved a very indifferent help, and did little more than look on. So vigorously, however, did she set to work, that by the next day the nest was nearly completed, and on the morning of the 27th, only three days after the nest-boxes had been put into the aviary, to the great joy of herself and our own children, she had deposited her first egg! Here was an event; the discovery of a new world by the Spanish seamen could scarcely have excited greater interest or curiosity than did the first glimpse of the little speckled globe now in our aviary. The thrilling rapture with which the first Crusaders gazed upon the battlements of the Holy City, or the wild delight with which the first settlers in the New World looked upon the Pacific Ocean, could scarcely exceed the delirious joy excited by this happy event in our youngsters' breasts. All were eager to have a peep at the long-expected treasure, though they knew they must not touch or tease the old bird with their inquisitiveness. To gratify this very pardonable curiosity, and as I knew they would not abuse it afterwards, I gave permission for them all to have a look. So, piling a number of boxes on the window-seat, they soon mounted up one after the other to satisfy their curiosity, and even Polly, the youngest, by standing on tiptoes, managed to get a glimpse of the precious gem, which having done they all set off to school with hearts as light and smiles as bright as the morning breeze. The next day poor little Blanche laid another, and the next another, then missing a day, the following morning, a fifth. So far all went merry as a marriage-bell, and our fondest hopes seemed in a fair way to be shortly realised. Others began to build

8

also, and by the Saturday following, Beauty and Buttercup had finished their nest, and on the Sunday morning the former had deposited her first egg therein. Little Blanche was indefatigable in her maternal duties, but her husband, I am sorry to say, who all along had shown himself to be only an idle, shacking sort of fellow, now exhibited himself in his true colours. Whenever she left the nest, instead of guarding it with jealous care against all marauders, as a good husband should, my gentleman began to pick out the soft cotton with which it was lined, and thus set a very bad example to the others, which, I am grieved to say, they were not slow to follow. For a day or two this sort of thing went on without any material harm being done, for, being an active, industrious little bird, little Blanche soon repaired the damage done in her absence, whilst she administered to the culprits caught in the act a sound drubbing, which they richly deserved. Often did they fly away with a flea in their ears for their wanton and malicious attacks upon other people's property, but alas! one morning we found the nest all turned upside down in the box, and though the eggs were not broken, and we tried to repair the damage, poor little Blanche looked the picture of misery, and never went near them again. Every now and then she would go and take a momentary peep at her now desolate house, but instinct, I suppose, told her that it would be useless to return. Her fondest hopes were evidently blighted, and the bright visions of her callei brood were at an end; and bitterly did she seem to mourn over her loss, whilst her good-for-

nothing husband looked on with the utmost indif-
ference. The eggs and nest were, after a day or two,
utterly left and deserted, and all was mute and blank
despair. As she sat upon her perch beside her rifled
home, she seemed to ask as many another bereaved
parent has done—

> " How can you bid this heart be blithe,
>   When blithe this heart can never be ?
> I've lost the jewel from my crown—
>   Look round our circle, and you'll see
> That there is ane out o' the ring
>   Who never can forgotten be.
> Ay, there's a blank at my right hand,
>   That ne'er can be made up to me.

> "'Tis said, as water wears the rock,
>   That time wears out the deepest line ;
> It may be true wi' hearts enow,
>   But never can apply to mine.
> For I have learned to know and feel
>   (Though losses should forgotten be)
> That still the blank at my right hand
>   Can never be made up to me.

> "I blame not Providence's sway,
>   For I have many joys beside ;
> And fain would I in grateful way
>   Enjoy the same, whate'er betide.
> A mortal thing should ne'er repine,
>   But stoop to God's supreme decree !
> Yet oh ! the blank at my right hand
>   Can never be made up to me !"

This was a very untoward and unlooked-for disaster,
but as it was clear there was no use in crying over spilt
milk or dwelling upon it in melancholy inactivity, after
a few days poor little Blanche set to work again as

industriously as ever, and soon regained her usual
good spirits. This time she selected a box in the very
opposite corner, and soon completed another nest as
quickly as before, whilst her mate, as if to make up
for his past misconduct, now began one on his own
account half way between the two. Each worked away
at its own box, paying an occasional visit to the
other, as though they were trying to see which could
make the best, but in no wise assisting in each other's
work. This certainly was very mysterious. What
could it mean? Did they intend to have a town and
country residence, or was one to be a cottage for the
children, whilst papa and mamma were attending to
their business at home? or did they intend to separate,
and have two distinct establishments, as some people
do who cannot agree to live together! This they did
not choose to inform us for the present; and so we
were left to our own conjecture and surmise. At times,
we thought Brilliant must be a hen, instead of a cock,
yet the brilliancy of his colour, his general appearance,
and his always being in the company of Blanche, forbad
the notion. Certainly it was curious that now they
should thus separate, and construct two habitations,
when only one could possibly be required. Hitherto,
every one who had seen him had considered him to be
a cock, and up to the time of making his first nest he
had been most assiduous in his attentions upon the
beautiful little Blanche. Day after day we watched
the denouement of this very mysterious business, and
wondered how it would ultimately end. Soon, it was
remarked, that master Spangle had suddenly become

suspiciously attentive to the fair Brilliant, and every day tended to confirm our worst surmises, when Judy got up to see what they were really doing with their nests, and descried three fine eggs in each! Our pet Brilliant had turned out an undoubted hen, and thus all our hopes of breeding London fancy birds with black wings and tail and pure golden bodies were for the time at an end! Nor was this the least part, or the whole of our misfortune; our whole arrangement in the upper aviary was altogether upset, for we had now two hens without a cock, and, in all probability, should soon have three, for master Spangle, there was too much reason to fear, would soon desert poor Lady Grey, of whom he had seemed passionately fond all the winter and spring. Of this danger she appeared to be aware, and so, thinking the best way to reclaim her recreant lord would be to build a nest herself, she immediately set to work and soon followed their example. Each lady then sat upon her own eggs without further molestation, and thus for a time harmony seemed to be restored, whilst at no distant date there appeared every probability that Mr. Spangle would have three wives on his hand, and a numerous family to support.

In this way time rolled on, when suddenly to our dismay the weather, from being warm and spring-like, became intensely cold, snow falling on the 12th of April, and ice forming in the night of considerable thickness. What, we naturally thought, would become of our young birds under such circumstances? The room in which they were was certainly as warm, or

even warmer than most ordinary rooms, but still it was
sufficiently cold, we knew, in the night time to give rise
to very serious apprehensions. We had already heard
some weeks past of young birds being hatched, and of
the almost hopeless endeavour to rear them, and now it
was colder than ever ! Well, we could not help it, the
eggs were laid, the birds were sitting, and the young
brood would soon be hatched in all human probability.
To provide flannel shirts for their little naked bodies
was impossible, and so they must take their chance.
As the expected day drew nigh when the first youngsters should break their shells and be introduced to the
light of day, all, as might be anticipated, began to be
eager to catch a first glimpse of the long-expected
treasures ! We had calculated our first birds would
make their appearance on the fourteenth ; but just as
we were on the point of starting for church the day
before, which happened to be Palm Sunday, Judy
rushed into the parlour in the highest state of excitement, saying, she was sure a young bird was hatched.
At first I doubted the fact, having calculated the period
of incubation, which lasts fourteen days, from the day
the last egg was laid.   In this, however, I was wrong,
the proper time being fourteen days from the first, each
egg being then consecutively hatched in the order they
are laid, which thus often makes two, three, and four
days' difference in the age of the birds.   She was sure
she had seen a small beak stretched out above Beauty's
nest to be fed, and was certain her eyes had not deceived
her.   Great was the joy which this startling intelli-
gence created amongst the children.   For a time they

could think of nothing else, so that I had some doubts as to the benefits they might get from the coming sermon. However, my misgivings were happily ill-founded, for on questioning them afterwards on the subject, though Judy confessed she could not help thinking about it whilst the bells were ringing, yet, as soon as the service commenced, she dismissed all thoughts of such things out of her head, and was able to join the service and follow the sermon throughout, as well as though nothing of the kind had happened. This was as it should be with us all at all times; and I need hardly say we all returned home with joyous hearts and happy feelings, without having allowed our earthly pleasures to interfere with our religious duties, or permitted our religious exercises to mar or cast a gloom upon our domestic pleasures, which surely God never intended they should do. In the afternoon, a second was said to have become visible, and now I hardly know which were the most pleased, the children or the parent birds. Beauty and Buttercup surveyed the little strangers with the fondness of a parent's eye, and evidently viewed them with the most exquisite delight. The news soon spread throughout the whole aviary that some young birds had been born into their little world, though no penny-a-liner connected with the press was there to publish it abroad. However, so it was; the secret was not to be kept long from the lady birds, who, we observed, immediately flocked round the happy pair, and had a peep at the little strangers, and, perhaps, congratulated their parents on their happy lot. Having done this, each returned to their respective homes, cheered, no doubt, and encouraged to further perseverance by the lovely sight, conscious that if they should only prove equally as attentive to their maternal duties as the happy pair before them, their labours would in due time be similarly blessed, and themselves be equally happy. Very cheering was it to watch these little birds constructing with artistic skill the soft lining of their nests; very lovely was it to notice the self-denying love and unwearied patience with which they brooded over their little eggs, and tended their caller-young. Beautifully and minutely has Erasmus Darwin sketched the whole process when describing that of their kindred finch, the linnet.

> " The busy birds, with nice selection, cull
> Soft thistle-down, grey moss, and scattered wool ;
> Far from each prying eye the nest prepare,
> Formed of warm moss, and lined with sóftest hair.
> Week after week, regardless of her food,
> Th' incumbent linnet warms her future brood ;
> Each spotted egg with 'vory bill she turns,
> Day after day with fond impatience burns—
> Hears the young prisoner chirping in his cell,
> And breaks in hemispheres the fragile shell !"

CHAPTER XVII.

OUR MISFORTUNES.

THOUGH one of our cocks had turned out a hen, and for the time disconcerted our plans, there was not a great deal the matter, seeing that we had now two nests full of eggs where we only expected to have had one. After all, we thought, we should have the best of the bargain, and already began to calculate our chickens, as usual, before they were hatched. In due time, however, this important preliminary to our success was brought about. Little Brilliant hatched two fine, strong, healthy-looking birds, whilst little Blanche had three equally promising. For a while they throve and increased; but just as they got well covered with pin-feathers all of a sudden they seemed to stop in their growth, becoming pale in hue instead of the red flesh colour which young birds in vigorous health always are, languished a day or two, and finally died. At first, we could not at all account for this singular retrograde movement, seeing that they were well supplied with excellent food, such as boiled egg chopped up very fine, and bread soaked in milk, besides the regular food for the old ones. On examination, however, which was further borne out by observation, we concluded that they really died of starvation, for they had nothing in their crops, and there could be no doubt but that the old birds from some cause or other had sadly neglected their tender offspring. It seems strange that any parent should willingly do this, and that amidst so much profusion and plenty, they should refuse to give to their young that food which instinct must tell them is absolutely necessary to sustain life. I do not suppose that such a thing often happens with birds in a wild state; but, I am sorry to say, it is a failing very prevalent amongst canaries in the tame, and that it is especially the case with the higher bred birds, who seem to have an especial aversion to any-thing like work. We thought we could account for our present disaster sufficiently well from the fact that both were hens without mates, and that as it was the duty of the ladies to sit on the eggs and hatch the young, so it became in turn the duty of the males to feed the birds so hatched, and that in point of fact this was to a great extent invariably left to their charge. Thus, the hens being left to themselves, and having no one to assist them in the very arduous duty of fill-ing so many little beaks perpetually opening and clamouring for food every time they returned to the nest, became tired of their ceaseless task, or followed the instinct of their nature and left off their maternal duties at the usual time, though they had no mates to take them up, and so the young birds suddenly stopped in their growth, languished a day or two, and finally died from sheer neglect and starvation. That such is the probable solution of the desertion of the young in the present case is, I think, very likely, though at the same time it is not altogether the reason I am equally satisfied, inasmuch as the same thing occurred to us over and over again where the hens had no such excuse, but where they and their lords proved equally remiss. As soon as we discovered that the old birds did not sufficiently feed them, we tried to supply their place by feeding them ourselves. In this work and labour of love, Judy bestowed great care and patience, getting up by four o'clock in the morning to feed them, but it was all to little purpose. If we had begun with them before they could see, perhaps we might have succeeded better, but now they could open their eyes it was very difficult to make them open their beaks and receive the food which we offered. They knew the difference between the hand that gave and the beak which should have brought them their necessary food, and, therefore, most pertinaceously refused to take it. We did all we could to surmount the difficulty, and were most anxious to supply the place of the parents, for the birds which we now had we could already see would be beautifully marked, and most rare in colour. Brilliant's were splendid golden-crested lizards, whilst one of little Blanche's was the most lovely and delicate fawn and white I ever beheld. Its head and wings were just the shade of that charming drab silk of which Quaker ladies twenty years ago seemed to enjoy an exclusive monopoly, but which their more fashionable successors appear to have almost entirely forsaken. For a time Judy's efforts seemed to prosper, and the bird to our great delight became almost fully fledged; but one bitter cold night she took it up to her bed-room in order to feed it as soon as it was light, when somehow

or other it got out of the flannel in which it was
wrapped, and was found dead when she awoke. The
others did not live so long, and thus all our hopes were
dashed to the ground, and so far as they were con-
cerned, there was little better prospect for the future.

The weather, as we said, had now turned bitterly
cold again, and for some time our Belgian-bred birds
showed no symptom of building. They were evidently
in no hurry to begin, but at length, about the middle of
April, the little green hen took the lead, and set the
others a good example by making a beautiful little
nest, and depositing therein four eggs. Like Beauty
and Buttercup above, she selected a box close to the
wires in one corner, whilst Daisy soon followed her
example by choosing the one adjacent at the back.
The latter laid five eggs, much finer and larger than
any we had yet had, whilst both were most attentive
to their maternal duties, scarcely leaving their nest
for food. This augured well for our success, and
anxiously did we count the days when the period of
incubation should be over, and more young birds
should be hatched. The tenth, eleventh, and twelfth
days passed away, the thirteenth dawned upon our
sight, when, horror of horrors, from some cause or
other, a fierce quarrel took place between these hitherto
peaceable birds, and the whole of the poor little green
hen's eggs were scattered on the ground, the very day
before they should and would have been hatched, for
they were all good. A second time did our little
green hen essay to redeem the misfortune of the past,
but with no better success than before. Again she

laid four eggs, but only succeeded in hatching two, which, like those of Brilliant and Blanche above, seemed to thrive and do very well until they had got well covered over with pin-feathers, so that we could see what colour they would be, when they, from some cause, suddenly stopped in their growth, languished and died. Though apparently excessively fond of them, neither she nor Dandy would feed them sufficiently, and so they died. A third time she made a nest, laid and hatched one young one, which perished in the same way, and then I thought she had done enough for one season, and so took her away from her lord. We had seen enough to show the unsoundness of the theory propounded by our German friend as to the colour of the offspring from two vivid green birds, for although one had a yellow mark on his back, all the others were undoubtedly green, thus showing that, after all, "like will produce like," not only in shape but colour.

By the beginning of June, Daisy and Marquis had completed their second nest, and the former safely deposited four more exceedingly fine eggs therein, which, after due time, were all hatched, producing four young birds. This was famous luck, and now we thought we should surely succeed, as Daisy, we did not doubt, would prove an exemplary mother. But alas! no, it was just as though an epidemic, or species of mania, had seized the birds; like the rest, after a few days, she seemed tired of feeding them, and her husband did not seem much inclined to supply her place. Thus they shared the same fate as the others, and out of this goodly nest-full, not one remained alive to increase our stock by the end of the following week.

In the upper aviary, our cinnamons gave equally as goodly promise, as did Daisy. Seraph and Sylph likewise completed their nest, and the latter laid four fine eggs, on which she duly sat, and then hatched, when Beauty made a marauding excursion to her nest, trying to steal the soft cotton therefrom, although there was plenty of fresh below for her especial use. A fierce battle accordingly ensued between these fair ladies, the consequence of which was most disastrous to the youthful birds, two of which were just hatched, both being kicked out of the nest in the fray, and drowned in the water-vase beneath. The nest was upset, and the remaining eggs were either broken or deserted, and thus our hopes in this direction were again frustrated, and our rarest coloured birds were desolate and forlorn. A second time they essayed, but with little better success. Two birds alone were hatched out of four eggs, but these were not sufficiently fed, and so they shared the same fate, notwithstanding all our efforts to the contrary. It was as though a spell hung over all our proceedings, and we were never to succeed in realising our fondly cherished dreams.

Our lizards did the worst of any, for Spangle, as we have already stated, deserted his lawful wife at the beginning, and took little notice of anything she did in the way of building. However she made an attempt notwithstanding, and laid two eggs, one of which got broken somehow, when she deserted the other and nest together. We put it under another hen who was sitting at the same time, but it came to nothing. For a long while poor Lady Grey seemed quite sad and forlorn, as well she might be to be so deserted by her husband, till at length we took them both out of the aviary together, and placed them in a breeding-cage by themselves. There she made another nest, but now became ill and out of health, so that she never laid again, and we took them with us into the country for change of air.

July came, and now we left town for our usual visit to the shires, and so ended all our hopes for the present year. Although our eight hens had laid upwards of eighty eggs, we only succeeded in rearing three birds, which, however, was enough to make us hope for better luck next time, and to keep us from despairing. Our misfortunes were chiefly owing to a series of untoward accidents, and we felt sure that as all our birds were young ones, and therefore having much to learn, they would become steadier and do better a second season. We therefore separated the cocks from the hens, placing each by themselves for the coming winter until spring should bring pairing-time again, when we hope for better luck and more prosperous times. Yes,

> " Sweet smile of hope, delicious tear,
>   The sun, the shower indeed shall come ;
>   The promised verdant shoots appear,
>   And nature bid her blossoms bloom."

We do not despair, but look forward with joy to the prospect of returning spring, when we may again essay

to realise our dreams of canary-breeding.   Thus it is
with us as it was with the farmer's boy—

> " Sunshine, health, and joy,
> Play round and cheer the elevated boy.
> ' Another spring !' his heart exulting cries ;
> ' Another year !' with promised blessings rise ;
> Eternal Power, from whom those blessings flow,
> Teach me still more to wonder, more to know ;
> Seed-time and harvest let me see again—
> Wander the leaf-strewn wood, the frozen plain,
> Let the first flower, corn-waving field, plain, tree,
> Here round my home, still lift my soul to Thee ;
> And let me ever, 'midst Thy bounties, raise
> An humble note of thankfulness and praise."

CHAPTER XVIII.

OUR INFIRMARY.

THE first patient we had under our care was the beautiful cinnamon bird, who, as we have already stated, was in a most deplorable state from dirt and neglect. The first thing we prescribed for her was the free use of the bath, of which she speedily and daily continued to avail herself. This soon effected a great change for the better in the general appearance of her plumage, but now a more serious matter demanded our attention. When she first came into our possession her feet were mere balls of dirt, which, though soon removed by the free use of the bath, so inflamed them that she could hardly put one foot to the ground. Indeed at night we discovered her frequently on the floor, panting and heaving with pain, sitting crumpled up in a corner instead of resting on a perch like her companions. We bathed her foot in warm water several times a day, and then dressed it with glycerine, at the same time mixing a few drops of aconite in her water to reduce the fever, which was considerable. Although the glycerine evidently did her foot good, yet we could not continue it, as it made such a mess with her feathers, to which it stuck most pertinaciously. We then tried spermaceti ointment, but this she invariably pecked off almost as soon as

9

applied. We then dressed it with arnica diluted in water, in the proportion of four or five drops of the former to half a teacupful of the latter, which soon had the desired effect. For a time the centre toe was quite stiff and useless, being swollen to twice the thickness of the others, but by degrees we reduced this by the arnica and the bathing, until at length a perfect cure was effected, and now she is one of the healthiest and cleanest, as well as most highly-prized birds in our aviary. Such a bad case as this can only happen through gross neglect and filthy habits; birds may sometimes have sore feet, however cleanly their apartments may be kept, and however well they may be supplied with water to bathe in, from the hardness of the old scales, but these may easily be softened and the soreness abated, by simply bathing them for five or ten minutes in warm water a few times in the day. In nine cases out of ten, this is all that will be found necessary, but if not, the treatment pursued above will soon effect a cure.

The next ailment that came under our notice was an attack of diarrhœa, which is a somewhat dangerous complaint, especially amongst high-bred birds. Happily for us, we had only one case, but it was the highest personage of our aviary, in fact no other than Sultan, the king of the Belgians. Like all the rest of his tribe, he was always, though very robust in his appearance, a very tender bird. The piercing cold of winter soon told tales about his constitution, and a severe attack of diarrhœa was the result. Fortunately we took it in time, and removed him to the hospital-

cage by himself, where we prescribed for him alternate
doses of rheum and mercurius, mixing four or five
drops of each in two separate vases of water. At the
same time we kept him very warm, supplying him
with boiled bread and milk, and other nourishing food,
which soon brought him round, and effected a cure.
We considered ourselves very fortunate, for great
numbers of birds are carried off annually by this
disease, which sometimes rages like an epidemic
amongst the feathered tribe, as it does in the human
race. The same treatment which is found most successful amongst the latter, will prove equally effectual
with birds. A little tincture of camphor dropped into
their water or on a lump of sugar, will also be of
service in the early stages, but if this fail, the prescrip-
tion above, I believe, will be found better than any of
the usual remedies ordinarily found in books, many of
which are as absurd as they are cruel.

The next case which called for immediate and decided
treatment was that of the Charming Princess, who,
after she had made her nest, we discovered to be egg-
bound. This was a dangerous case brought on by the
sudden change in the weather, which just then became
as nipping as the coldest day in winter. She was a
long while making her nest, occupying more than a
week over what some of her companions would have
finished in a couple of days. However it was completed at last, when we observed she began to look
poorly, crouching down to the ground, or sitting all of
a heap on the perches. No egg was laid, and she
appeared day after day to get visibly worse, until we

came to the conclusion that she could not lay, or in other words, was egg-bound. This, as we have said, was a dangerous state of things, and necessitated an immediate remedy, for if not speedily relieved, inflammation would set in, and death must inevitably ensue. Mere alterations in diet, as often recommended in such cases, we knew would not only be useless, but highly dangerous, seeing that the malady might run its course ere these could possibly produce any effect. Accordingly we adopted a very simple and efficacious plan which rarely or ever fails to produce the desired result, viz., a little castor-oil applied in the following manner. Taking a penny camel-hair paint brush, and working it into a point, we dipped it into some castor-oil, and gently inserted it gradually up the vent of the bird, applying a little outside as well, over the part affected to allay any inflammation which might exist, and at the same time putting a drop or so in its beak. The next morning we found an egg safely deposited in the nest, which of course relieved us of all further anxiety about the case. We have since tried the same plan on several others, and invariably with the same result. Indeed Mr. M— tells us, so sure a remedy is it, that no one need lose a bird from this cause ; we can, therefore, confidently recommend it to others, whose birds may be affected with what is generally considered a very serious, and often fatal disease

The next disorder that came under our notice was a very insidious one, of which we knew not for some time either the existence or the cause. For a long time we observed two of our Belgian birds, who, compared with other breeds, are of most indolent habits, to be getting daily rougher in their feathers, and to begin to shed those of the wing until the pinions became quite bare and red. What was the matter we could not tell, and, therefore, what to do we were entirely at a loss, until we accidentally met with a small German pamphlet on piping bullfinches, which at once explained the mystery. By this, we discovered our birds were infested with a number of small red lice, nearly invisible to the naked eye, but which often become so numerous as to suck their blood to such an extent that they not only speedily become emaciated, but even died. Various remedies I have since found are recommended in various books, such as a pinch of Scotch snuff sprinkled under the wing and which at best can but afford partial relief. The one I adopted I feel convinced to be the best, though I should only recommend it to be used by a grown up person, as the solution is a deadly poison, which may prove not only fatal to the bird but to others if carelessly left about. Dissolving a pennyworth of white precipitate powder into half a teacupful of warm water, I made a solution with which by means of a small brush I dressed each bird thoroughly all over, taking especial care that the mixture did not get either into his mouth or eyes. Then washing the whole off with soap and warm water, I wrapped the bird in a piece of flannel, and laid it before the fire until it was partially dry, when I placed it in a cage covered over with the same material, keeping it still before the fire until it was thoroughly comfortable as before. They looked wretched objects for a time, indeed so much so that Judy quite thought the first we did would never recover, and pleaded hard for the rest going undone. I myself had some misgivings as to the result, but the warm flannel and comfortable fire soon dried their saturated feathers, so that before night we might say of each "Richard was himself again." The next day the birds became quite cheerful and lively, and our only regret was that we had not discovered the disorder, and applied the remedy before. We have since repeated the application to every bird in our aviary after the breeding season was over, when we found some of the nest boxes to be swarming with these living pests, and with very manifest advantage and success. Instead of using a brush, however, we found it easier and quicker and more effectual, to dip the bird bodily into the solution at once, taking care as before that none might get into its beak or eyes, and then into a basin of warm water as before. All birds, it is said, are infested more or less with these nasty vermin, but generally manage to keep them down by frequent bathing and dusting themselves in sand. This I can imagine to be true, for all the other birds at this time were clean and healthy, and in good feather, having bathed daily throughout the winter. These, however, had been indolent and inactive, seldom or ever either bathing or pluming themselves, even in the finest weather, thus proving beyond the shadow of a doubt that in birds, as well as in human beings, idleness and dirty habits will inevitably bring on misery, and disease, and death. To be healthy, we must be both cleanly in our persons and active in our bodies; these combined will give energy to the limbs and tone to the mind, which, together with plain and nutritious food we take to be the great secret of health.

The only other case which came under our treatment was a case of asthma, which, as already stated, we failed to cure. Bechstein says that it is a disease easily cured; for my own part I doubt the fact. The remedies we used were those generally prescribed for the human patient, and for a time they seemed to afford a temporary relief. The disease, however, appeared to us to be untouched, and to return with every vicissitude of the weather. Our bird, so long as she remained under our immediate care did well enough, and might probably have lived a long while; but a few weeks in other hands, without the special attention she had with us, sufficed to seal her fate. The remedies we tried were the homœopathic preparation of ipecacuanha, phosphorus, bryonia, and sulphur, in tinctures of the first dilution; but though some appeared to give relief for a time, they did not effect a cure. I have seen many birds similarly affected, and variously treated but with the same result. Still Bechstein says " a favorite linnet and goldfinch when attacked with very bad asthma, were relieved and preserved for several years by the following method. The first thing was entirely to leave off hemp-seed, reducing them to rape-seed only; but giving them at the same time abundance of bread soaked in pure water and then pressed; lettuce, endive or watercresses, according to the seasons, twice a week, giving them boiled bread and milk about the size of a nutmeg. This is made by throwing a piece of the crum of white bread, about the size of a nut, into a teacupful of milk, boiling it and stirring it all the time with a wooden spoon till it is of the consistency of pap. It must be quite cold before it is given to the birds, and must always be made fresh, for if sour it will prove injurious. This paste, which they are very fond of, purges them sufficiently, and sensibly relieves them./ In very violent attacks nothing but this paste ought to be given for two or three days following, and this will soon give the desired relief. When the disease is only slight or only begun, it is sufficient to give the bread and milk once in three or four days. When employed under similar circumstances this treatment has cured several very valuable birds." We give the remedy as we find it, as it is one easily tried, but we ourselves have little faith in its efficacy, if the disease be anything but a temporary effect of some external cause, such as the giving of too much hemp-seed or the exposure to too much heat, which, of course, will vanish with the removal of the cause. Beyond this, we doubt whether there be any cure for a disease which has its seat in the delicate organs of the throat and chest, and which though relieved almost invariably lasts as long as the patient is alive, whether it be man, bird, or beast.

This completed the list of cases in our infirmary, and these, under ordinary circumstances, will be found to be the chief ailments of the canary. The medicines we used were the homœopathic tinctures, which are far more convenient and efficacious than any other form of medicine for the feathered tribe. As we have proved their efficacy in the case of man and beast for many years, we can confidently recommend their use to others. Canaries, though to a certain extent tender birds, require little in the way of medicine. Only give them plenty of good sound canary and rape seed, with now and then a little hemp as a treat, and not as their general food ; a little green food, such as lettuce, mustard and cress, or apple or boiled carrot according to the season, with plenty of clean water and red sand to bathe and dust themselves in, and you will have little trouble about doctoring. Provided you keep them in an equal temperature, away from all cold draughts of air, than which nothing kills them sooner, in a light cheerful cage in which there is plenty of room, and where there is the cheering warmth of the morning sun, no birds will be found hardier or require less care or attention. We would advise no one, however, to keep canaries, or, indeed, any other bird or animal that is deprived of the means of taking care of itself, who is not really naturally fond of such things, for if it be only taken up from fashion, or through a momentary whim, depend upon it after the novelty is over, the attention they require will soon become a trouble, and the trouble will cause neglect, and neglect will cause much misery and suffering, if not actual death to the once charming pet. No, to take a real pleasure in such things you must be " born, as it were, to love pigs and poultry ;" it is a taste which cannot be acquired, but being innate, will cause the necessary trouble it entails to be a pleasure, and the care "a work and labour of love."

CHAPTER XIX.

ON CAGES.

CAGES suitable and proper for a canary are not altogether so much mere matters of taste as some people are apt to imagine. They may be too small or too large, too ornamental or too elaborate in their workmanship, and in either or all of these cases they do not answer the purpose required. If a cage be too small it is cruel to the bird you desire to pet, while if it be too large, a single bird will not only appear lost in it, but in all probability it will have the effect of making him less disposed to treat you with his song. On the other hand, if a cage be too elaborate and ornamental in its design and workmanship, the effect will be to fasten the attention rather on the casket than on the jewel it is meant to enshrine. Since the first Great Exhibition in Hyde Park we have had bird-cages of every form and description. Swiss cottages, Chinese pagodas, Gothic churches, and Indian temples, with their painted domes and minarets, all doing great credit to the taste and enterprise of our workers in tin, but utterly unadapted to the purpose required. To do this satisfactorily we maintain that the cage should always be subordinate to the bird, and its main object be to set off to the greatest advantage the plumage of the latter, and just in proportion as it

does this will it come up to our *beau ideal* of what a
cage should be. Whenever we see a beautiful canary
imprisoned in one of these gorgeously got up gimcracks
of zinc, we always feel very much what an artist in
some picture exhibition, standing near his own produc-
tion to hear the criticisms of the public, may be supposed to feel, as he hears some unsophisticated party
exclaim, "Oh, my! what a beautiful frame!" No,
this is surely putting the cart before the horse, and
therefore at once disposes of all these pretty toys, as
fit and proper habitations for our pet. No one who
has had a bird fit to be called a canary will ever
hide him in one of these, whilst those who possess
the lowest kind of the species only will hardly think
them to be worthy of so expensive a domicile.

For single birds the two cages we should recommend are the japanned bell-shaped cage, and the plain
square white tinned sort. The former is light, airy
and elegant, and answers well for a single bird, who
always looks well in it. It has the recommendation of
being easily cleaned, and of affording the least possible
screen for those pests and scourges of the canary, red-
lice. The only drawback is, that its shape precludes
it from being hung up against a wall, but for a stand,
or to be suspended from a ceiling nothing can be better
for the purpose. In this, as in all other wares, there
are inferior kinds, of which I would fain put my readers
on their guard, for the cheaper imitations of the real
article being badly japanned and painted with the
worst of paint, and therefore easily picked off, as we
have experienced to our sorrow, are often the unsus-

pected cause of ill-health, and death of many a valued and valuable bird. Of course the only way to guard against this disaster is to go to the best makers, or the leading bird-dealers, who are sure to patronise the best articles.

But the cage to set off a canary to the greatest advantage, and which therefore we recommend before all others, is the plain square-topped cage, made of white tin wire without any wood-work at all, except the bottom, which should be of polished ebony, or at least, if of other wood, stained black. This suits alike all birds of whatever colour they may be, but we need hardly say sets off the pale yellow or the deep orange to the very greatest advantage. It is far beyond the common mahogany, as any one may judge for himself if he will only contrast any substance of red and yellow together, beside yellow and black. All fanciers when they wish to exhibit their birds to a purchaser or otherwise, invariably use a black cage and not a mahogany one, which speaks for itself. And yet how few such cages do you see exhibited for sale; if you wish for one, it is ten to one that you will have specially to order it, and yet its greater superiority for exhibiting a canary off to the best advantage over all the japanned pagodas and Swiss cottages that ever were made is beyond dispute, and requires only to be seen to be at once admitted.

For the purpose of breeding of course a cage of a totally different construction is required, and the ordinary shape will answer every end. The double one, however, will probably be most convenient, its size being something like the following dimensions, viz., three feet six inches long, one foot wide, and two feet high. This will be quite large enough, divided by a wooden partition in the centre, for two pair of birds, and it will be far better in the end to have a number of these according to the extent of your breeding establishment, than to put two or more pairs together in a larger cage, as they are almost sure to fight, when the hazard of breaking their eggs, or killing the young, we need scarcely say, is very great. Under any circumstances we hold prevention to be far better than cure, and even if we had a room at our disposal for the purpose, we should prefer a number of separate cages or compartments for each pair of birds, rather than turn them into it promiscuously. We speak from our own experience in this matter, and confidently recommend a separate cage such as we have described above, to all who wish to unite the greatest amount of success with the minimum of disaster.

When the young birds are to be weaned, or when a number of old birds, after the breeding season is over, have to be kept together, a third cage of a still different construction is required. This is an oblong wire cage of goodly size, according to the number of birds to be put into it, and sufficiently large for the young birds to fly about in, and exercise the muscles of their wings and body. This is a matter of the very greatest importance, for without exercise, and strong exercise too, young birds can never be healthy or strong. Our own cage is of the following dimensions, and one of the best for the purpose we have seen, viz., four feet long, eighteen inches wide, and twenty-two inches high. Every one may not have room enough for so large a cage, but the nearer their cage approaches these dimensions, most assuredly the better it will be for their young birds. These cannot have too much room for exercise, and on the quantity they are able to get when first taken away from their parents, will their health and vigour greatly depend.

Possessing cages of the several kinds we have described, you will have every requisite necessary for the exhibition, breeding, and weaning of your canaries. In any case, whether you have one or all, be sure that the wire of which they are made be not brass, for this produces verdigris which I need scarcely say, if eaten, will be fatal to your pets. Let the drinking font be the pear-shaped glass font, which is ever self-supplying and whose neck being inside the cage will preserve your birds from the risk of being left without water. For the ordinary seed I recommend the open drawer, with a smaller one for a little hemp or other dainty. These with a tin pan for sopped bread, or egg in breeding-time will complete the fittings-up of your cages, and leave nothing to be desired.

With this advice, and hoping my readers may profit by the experience set forth in these pages, I will now bid them Farewell.

FAREWELL.

"Thou 'rt bearing hence thy roses,
  Glad summer, fare thee well!
Thou 'rt singing thy last melodies
  In every wood and dell.

"But ere the golden sunset
  Of thy latest lingering day,
Oh! tell me, o'er this chequered earth,
  How hast thou passed away?

"Brightly, sweet summer, brightly
  Thine hours have floated by,
To the joyous birds of the woodland boughs,
  The rangers of the sky.

"And brightly in the forests
  To the wild deer wandering free;
And brightly 'mid the garden flowers
  To the happy murmuring bee.

"But how to human bosoms,
  With all their hopes and fears,
And thoughts that make their eagle-wings
  To pierce the unborn years?

Sweet summer! to the captive
   Thou hast flown in burning dreams
Of the woods, with all their whispering leaves,
   And the blue rejoicing streams;

"To the wasted and the weary,
   On the bed of sickness bound,
In swift delirious fantasies,
   That changed with every wound;

" To the sailor on the billows,
   In longings wild and vain
For the gushing founts and breezy hills,
   And the homes of earth again!

" And unto me, glad summer,
   How hast thou flown to me!
My chainless footsteps naught hath kept
   From thy haunts of song and glee!

" Thou hast flown in wayward visions,
   In memories of the dead—
In shadows from a troubled heart
   O'er thy sunny pathway shed.

" In brief and sudden strivings
   To fling a weight aside—
'Midst these thy melodies have ceased,
   And all thy roses died.

" But oh, thou gentle summer!
   If I greet thy flowers once more,
Bring me again the buoyancy
   Wherewith my soul should soar.

10

" Give me to hail thy sunshine,
    With song and spirit free ;
Or in a purer air than this
    May that next meeting be."

PRINTED BY J. E. ADLARD, BARTHOLOMEW CLOSE, E.C.

Crown 8vo, elegantly bound, cloth gilt, Illustrated with 8 beautifully coloured full-page Plates and 90 Wood Engravings, price 3s. 6d.

FIELD FLOWERS

A HANDY BOOK

FOR

THE RAMBLING BOTANIST,

SUGGESTING

WHAT TO LOOK FOR AND WHERE TO GO IN THE OUT-DOOR STUDY OF

BRITISH PLANTS.

BY SHIRLEY HIBBERD, F.R.H.S.

"It will serve as an excellent introduction to the practical study of wild flowers."—*The Queen.*

"We cannot praise too highly the illustrations which crowd the pages of this handbook; the coloured plates are especially attractive, and serve to bring before us very distinctly the most prominent flowers of the field, the heaths, and the hedgerows."—*Examiner.*

GROOMBRIDGE & SONS, 5, Paternoster Row, London.

Crown 8vo, elegantly bound, cloth gilt, illustrated with 8 beautifully coloured Plates and 40 Wood Engravings, price 3s. 6d.

THE FERN GARDEN

HOW TO MAKE, KEEP, AND ENJOY IT

OR,

FERN CULTURE MADE EASY.

BY SHIRLEY HIBBERD, F.R.H.S.

CONTENTS.

FERNS IN GENERAL
FERN COLLECTING
HOW TO FORM AN OUTDOOR FERNERY
CULTIVATION OF ROCK FERNS
CULTIVATION OF MARSH FERNS
FERNS IN POTS
THE FERN HOUSE
THE FERNERY AT THE FIRESIDE

MANAGEMENT OF FERN CASES
THE ART OF MULTIPLYING FERNS
BRITISH FERNS
CULTIVATION OF GREENHOUSE STOVE FERNS
SELECT GREENHOUSE FERNS
SELECT STOVE FERNS
TREE FERNS
FERN ALLIES

GROOMBRIDGE & SONS, 5, Paternoster Row, London.

BOOKS FOR YOUNG NATURALISTS.

Crown 8vo, elegantly bound, gilt edges, Illustrated with 16 beautifully coloured Plates and numerous Wood Engravings, price 5s.

NESTS AND EGGS
OF FAMILIAR BIRDS.

Described and Illustrated with an account of the Haunts and Habits of the Feathered Architects, and their Times and Modes of Building.

By H. G. ADAMS.

GROOMBRIDGE & SONS, 5, Paternoster Row, London.

Crown 8vo, elegantly bound, gilt edges, Illustrated with 8 beautifully coloured Plates and numerous Wood Engravings, price 3s. 6d.

BEAUTIFUL BUTTERFLIES.
DESCRIBED AND ILLUSTRATED

With an Introductory chapter, containing the History of a Butterfly through all its Changes and Transformations. A Description of its Structure in the Larva, Pupa, and Imago states, with an Explanation of the scientific terms used by Naturalists in reference thereto, with observations upon the Poetical and other associations of the Insect.

By H. G. ADAMS.

GROOMBRIDGE & SONS, 5, Paternoster Row, London.

Crown 8vo, elegantly bound, gilt edges, Illustrated with 8 beautifully coloured Plates and numerous Wood Engravings, price 3s. 6d.

BEAUTIFUL SHELLS
THEIR NATURE, STRUCTURE, AND USES
FAMILIARLY EXPLAINED.

With Directions for Collecting, Clearing and Arranging them in the Cabinet.

Descriptions of the most remarkable Species, and of the creatures which inhabit them, and explanations of the meaning of their scientific names, and of the terms used in Conchology.

By H. G. ADAMS.

GROOMBRIDGE AND SONS, 5, Paternoster Row, London.

Crown 8vo, elegantly bound, gilt edges, Illustrated with 8 beautifully coloured Plates and Wood Engravings, price 3s. 6d.

HUMMING BIRDS.
DESCRIBED AND ILLUSTRATED.
WITH AN

Introductory Sketch of their Structure, Plumage, Haunts, Habits, etc.

By H. G. ADAMS.

GROOMBRIDGE & SONS, 5, Paternoster Row, London.

Crown 8vo., cloth gilt.   Illustrated with Coloured Plates and Wood Engravings.   Price 3s. 6d.

SKETCHES

OF

BRITISH INSECTS

A HANDBOOK FOR BEGINNERS IN THE STUDY OF ENTOMOLOGY.

BY REV. W. HOUGHTON, M.A., F.L.S.

Author of "Country Walks of a Naturalist," "Sea-side Walks of a Naturalist," etc., etc.

The object of this volume is to give a short sketch of our British Insects, with the hope of inducing dwellers in the country to take an interest in these winged denizens of the air, and to enable the reader to acquire a general knowledge of insect life, as exhibited in the fields and lanes of the country.

GROOMBRIDGE & SONS, 5, Paternoster Row, London.

Crown 8vo., cloth, gilt edges.   Illustrated with Coloured Plates and Wood Engravings.   Price 3s. 6d.

THE

DWELLERS IN OUR GARDENS

THEIR LIVES AND WORKS.

BY SARA WOOD.

CONTENTS :

GROOMBRIDGE & SONS, 5, Paternoster Row, London.